Pride and Prejudice

Jane Austen

Simplified and abridged by

MANJU SAMBHUNATH SEN

Consultant editor

Bikram K. Das
Formerly:
Professor, Central Institute of English and Foreign Languages, Hyderabad
Professor, National Institute of Education, Singapore and Director,
English Language Teaching Institute, Bhubaneswar

With a special introduction by

Meenakshi Mukherjee
Formerly Professor of English
Jawaharlal Nehru University, Delhi

Orient BlackSwan

PRIDE AND PREJUDICE

ORIENT BLACKSWAN PRIVATE LIMITED

Registered Office
3-6-752, Himayatnagar, Hyderabad 500 029, Telangana, India
e-mail: centraloffice@orientblackswan.com

Other Offices
Bengaluru, Bhopal, Chennai, Guwahati, Hyderabad, Jaipur,
Kolkata, Lucknow, Mumbai, New Delhi, Noida, Patna, Visakhapatnam

First published under Orient Longman Easy Readers Series 2003
First Published under Orient Longman Undergraduate Text 2007
First Orient Blackswan Impression 2008
Reprinted 2009, 2019

ISBN: 978 81 250 3249 6

Typeset in ElegaGarmond BT 12/14 by
OSDATA, Hyderabad 500 029

Printed in India at
Deepak Pustak Bandhnalaya
Delhi

Published by
Orient Blackswan Private Limited
3-6-752, Himayatnagar,
Hyderabad 500 029 (Telangana), INDIA
e-mail: info@orientblackswan.com

INTRODUCTION

I

One of the pleasures shared by people everywhere in the world—adults and children alike—is reading or listening to stories or watching them on the screen. Whether it is a book or a film or a television serial or a grandmother narrating a tale, it is always the curiosity about 'what happened next' that holds our attention. The story may be about places we know and familiar characters that we see around us every day or it may be about distant lands and people who live differently, but if narrated well, it will create the same interest. That is true about time as well. *The Ramayana* is set in a very remote past—thousands of years ago—but a child enjoys the adventures of Hanuman as much as that of Harry Potter who is supposed to be living in England today. The magic of a good story can work across time and place.

The printed page has been the most popular medium through which people have responded to stories. Nothing can replace the joy of reading a book because this is an activity one can engage in alone, anywhere and anytime and without the help of technology. Unlike watching television which makes one completely passive, the process of reading demands the reader's active involvement. While reading a story the reader's imagination creates pictures in the mind: hence the writer and reader become equal partners in bringing the story alive. Once one gets into the habit, not only does reading become a life-long source of pleasure but it opens out windows to unknown lands and new experiences.

The present novel *Pride and Prejudice* was published nearly two hundred years ago (1813) in London and it has continued to be popular wherever the English language is used. It has also been translated into many other languages. Since 1940 three Hollywood films and two TV serials have been made based on this story, the most recent being a film version made in 2005 which was nominated for a number of Academy Awards. The story is about a family of five lively sisters, their parents, neighbours, friends, and the young men they meet in the course of one year. The novel ends with three marriages and a promise of happiness for everyone. I suggest you look at the rest of the Introduction only after reading the novel so that you can compare your impressions of the book with the points made here.

II

Jane Austen (1775–1817), the writer of *Pride and Prejudice,* lived a quiet life in the green and pastoral south of England before industrialisation had altered the landscape. She did not travel much and wrote from the experience of what she saw around her. Life in a small English town those days had a slow pace and most of the residents knew each other. The landed upper class families had leisure and social interactions like parties, balls, picnics formed an important part of their lives. Clothes and manners were considered important in creating an impression. Jane Austen was an acute and amused observer of human behaviour and all the six novels she wrote in her short life of forty-two years continue to delight readers even now because of her wit, humour and an ability to weave a captivating story out of ordinary incidents. Love and marriage are very often her central themes but if one reads carefully one notices the many layers of irony and social comment that exist in these seemingly simple tales.

The very first sentence of the novel *Pride and Prejudice* illustrates this irony and sets the tone for the novel: 'It is a truth universally acknowledged that a single man in possession of a good fortune must be in want of a wife.' We know, as the author does, that it is not a truth, let alone a universal one. The young man in question may not feel the want, but the society around him, particularly the parents of marriageable daughters would like him to feel it because it would suit their interest. The sentence points indirectly toward the hard truth that marriage is not so much about love and romance as about money and property. Whenever an eligible young man is introduced in the novel we are generally informed about his financial position. Mr Bingley's 'large fortune' and Mr Darcy's 'ten thousand pounds a year' make them specially desirable in social gatherings where young men and women meet.

But does Jane Austen really think money is all that matters in human relationships? If she did, she would not have created a free and natural character such as Elizabeth Bennett and place her at the centre of the novel *Pride and Prejudice*. In a society which pays too much attention to wealth and manners Elizabeth Bennett stands out as a spirited and intelligent young woman who does not care much for public opinion. Even though women in her class were not supposed to go anywhere alone, Elizabeth decides to walk three miles in bad weather to meet her sister who is ill and stranded in Mr Bingley's house. When she arrives, Mr Bingley's fashionable sisters are shocked by her muddy shoes and dirty stockings, but that does not bother Elizabeth.

Elizabeth generally values a man not for his income but for his personal qualities. This is particularly remarkable because her father is not rich and in any case by the law of the land his property was not to be inherited by his daughters but by the nearest male heir. This was particularly hard on the girls because in the families of English gentry those days, women did not have the option of earning their livelihood independently. Hence marriage was their only way of acquiring financial security. Elizabeth knew very well that she would not be able to survive without marriage. Yet in the course of the novel we see her refusing two marriage proposals – one from Mr Collins who would have provided her with a comfortable home if nothing else, and one from Mr Darcy, one of the richest bachelors in the country and the master of a large and beautiful estate. She does not like Mr Collins because he is pompous and behaves in a silly and artificial manner; and she is put off by the pride of Mr Darcy. Elizabeth is disappointed that her best friend accepts the insufferable Mr Collins as husband because she might not have a better offer.

By the end of the novel when Darcy proposes to Elizabeth the second time and Elizabeth accepts, much has happened to make Darcy a better human being in Elizabeth's eyes and convince her that he is a man she can respect. He has shown himself to be a caring and helpful person, responsible as a brother and kind to those who work for him. He had lost the arrogance that he had when Elizabeth had seen him for the first time.

Not only money but social class is another factor by which people were valued in the society Jane Austen was writing about. In *Pride and Prejudice* we see people like Mr Collins and the Lucas family being excessively respectful to Lady Catherine de Bourgh simply because of her title. Only Elizabeth has the courage to stand up to her when she makes patronising comments about her education in Chapter 9. And later in chapter 19 when Lady Catherine insults Elizabeth by saying she should not by aspire to marry Darcy because he belongs to a higher class, Elizabeth retorts: 'he (Darcy) is a gentleman; I am a gentleman's daughter: so far we are equal.' We notice that in those days the landed gentry who did not have to work for their living had a prejudice against people who were in trade or any other profession like law, but by the end of the novel Darcy is mature enough to accept people for what they are as human beings rather than judge them by their class or profession. The novel ends with a reference to Darcy's intimacy with the Gardiners, a couple he would not have cared to know earlier because they were not people with land and property. We cannot help thinking that Elizabeth is partly responsible for bringing about this change in Darcy.

Today we read *Pride and Prejudice* not only because the author introduces us to a certain kind of British society and lets us see through its pretensions, but mainly because she creates characters who engage our interest or amuse us by their follies. Gushing Mrs Bennet with her one- point agenda of getting her daughters married anyhow and quiet Mr Bennet with his caustic humour make a believable pair who could easily have been our neighbours in an Indian town. The difference among the sisters—beautiful but mild Jane with a willingness to please everybody, sharp Elizabeth with a mind of her own who can score a point by giving a witty answer, giddy Lydia who would run after any man in a military uniform—come alive through their individual characteristics. Jane Austen's novel is rooted in its place and time—England two centuries ago—but readers in India today can easily recognise the human qualities that make her characters real for all time.

Meenakshi Mukherjee

CONTENTS

1

THE BENNETS OF LONGBOURN

It is a truth universally accepted that a single man in possession of a good fortune must be in want of a wife. However little known the feelings of such a man may be on his first entering a neighbourhood, he is considered the rightful property of some one or other of the daughters of the surrounding families.

"My dear Mr Bennet," said his wife to him one day, "have you heard that Netherfield Park is let at last?"

Mr Bennet replied that he had not.

"But it is," she returned, "for Mrs Long has just been here, and she told me all about it."

Mr Bennet didn't answer.

"Don't you want to know who has taken it?" cried his wife.

"*You* want to tell me, and I have no objection to hearing it."

This was invitation enough.

"Mrs Long says that Netherfield is taken by a young man of large fortune from the north of England, that he came down on Monday to see the house and was so delighted with it that he agreed to take possession immediately."

"What is his name?"

"Bingley."

"Is he married or single?"

"Oh! Single, my dear, to be sure! A single man of large fortune; four or five thousand a year. What a fine thing for our girls!"

"How so? What can it matter to them?"

"My dear Mr Bennet," replied his wife, "how can you be so tiresome! You must know that I am thinking of his marrying one of them."

"Is that his intention in settling here?"

"Intention! Nonsense, how can you talk so! But it is very likely that he *may* fall in love with one of them, and therefore you must visit him as soon as he comes."

"I see no reason for that. You and the girls may go, or you may send them by themselves."

"But, my dear, you must certainly go and see Mr Bingley when he comes."

"It is more than I promise, I assure you."

"But consider your daughters. Only think what an excellent marriage it would be for one of them. Sir William and Lady Lucas have decided to go just for that reason. Indeed you must go, for it will be impossible for *us* to visit him, if you do not."

"Why should you be so particular? I dare say that Mr Bingley will be very glad to see you, and I will send a few lines by you to assure him of my hearty consent to his marrying whichever he chooses of the girls; though I must put in a good word for my little Lizzy."

"I desire you will do no such thing. Lizzy is not a bit better than the others; she is not half so good-looking as Jane, nor half so good-humoured as Lydia."

"They are all silly and ignorant, like other girls," he replied. "But Lizzy is rather more intelligent than her sisters."

"Mr Bennet, how can you talk about your own children in such a way? You take delight in annoying me. You have no pity on my poor nerves."

"You mistake me, my dear. I have a great respect for your nerves. I have heard you mention them these twenty years."

"Ah! You do not know what I suffer."

Mr Bennet was a strange mixture of great intelligence, sarcastic humour, and reserve. He seldom showed his feelings. The experience of twenty-three years had not been sufficient to make his wife understand his character. She was neither clever nor sensible nor good-humoured. When she was discontented, she fancied herself nervous. The business of her life was to get her daughters married; her amusement was visiting others and gathering news.

Mr Bennet was among the earliest of those who called on Mr Bingley. He had always intended to visit him but revealed it only on the following morning. Observing his second daughter trimming a hat, he suddenly spoke to her,

"I hope Mr Bingley will like it, Lizzy."

"How are we to know *what* Mr Bingley likes," said her mother angrily, "since we are not to visit him."

"But you forget, mamma," said Elizabeth, "that we shall meet him at the balls, and that Mrs Long has promised to introduce him."

"I do not believe that Mrs Long will do any such thing, since she has two nieces of her own."

"I am glad to find that you do not depend on her serving you," said Mr Bennet.

Mrs Bennet decided not to reply.

"When is your next ball to be, Lizzy?"

"Tomorrow fortnight."

"So it is," cried her mother, "and Mrs Long does not come back till the day before; so, it will be impossible for her to introduce him, for she will not know him herself."

"Then, my dear, you may introduce Mr Bingley to *her*."

---

sarcastic: making bitter remarks, intended to hurt someone's feelings
trimming: decorating
ball: a social gathering, especially arranged, where couples dance together for pleasure

"Impossible, Mr Bennet, impossible, when I am not acquainted with him myself."

"Well, if you refuse, I will take it on myself."

The girls stared at their father. Mrs Bennet said only, "Nonsense, nonsense, I am sick of Mr Bingley."

"Why did you not tell me so before? If I had known as much this morning, I certainly would not have called on him."

The astonishment of the ladies was just what he wished. Presently Mrs Bennet said that it was what she had expected all the while. "I was sure you loved your girls too well to neglect such an acquaintance."

"What an excellent father you have, girls!" said Mrs Bennet. "Lydia, my love, though you *are* the youngest, I dare say Mr Bingley will dance with you at the next ball."

"Oh!" said Lydia. "I am not afraid: for though I am the youngest I *am* the tallest."

The rest of the evening was spent in wondering how soon Mr Bingley would return Mr Bennet's visit and deciding when they should ask him to dinner.

2

THE NEW NEIGHBOUR

All Mrs Bennet's questions, and those of her five daughters, could not draw from her husband any satisfactory description of Mr Bingley. They had to accept the highly favourable report of their neighbour, Lady Lucas. He was quite young, wonderfully handsome, extremely agreeable and to crown everything he meant to be at the next ball with a large party.

In a few days Mr Bingley returned Mr Bennet's visit. He had hopes of seeing the young ladies, of whose beauty he had heard much; but he saw only the father. An invitation to dinner was sent soon afterwards; but Mr Bingley sent an answer that he had to be in town the next day and was unable to accept their invitation. Mrs Bennet was most upset, but Lady Lucas suggested that he might have gone to London only to get a large party for the ball.

When the party entered the ball room, it consisted of only five altogether: Mr Bingley, his two sisters, the husband of the elder, Mr Hurst, and another young man. Mr Bingley was good-looking and gentlemanly; he had a pleasant expression, and easy manners. His sisters looked very fashionable. His friend, Mr Darcy, soon drew the attention of the room by his fine tall appearance, handsome features and the report of his having ten thousand a year. He was looked at with great admiration

---

to crown everything: to make a perfect ending

for about half the evening, but his manners turned the tide of his popularity; for he was found to be proud and disagreeable.

Mr Bingley soon acquainted himself with all the people in the room. He talked of giving a ball himself at Netherfield. What a contrast there was between him and his friend! Mr Darcy danced once with Mrs Hurst and once with Miss Bingley, refused to be introduced to any other lady, and spent the rest of the evening in walking about the room. As there were not enough gentlemen, Elizabeth had to sit down without a partner for two dances. During part of that time, Mr Darcy had been standing near enough for her to overhear a conversation between him and Mr Bingley.

"Come, Darcy," said Bingley, "why do you stand about by yourself in this stupid manner? You had much better dance."

"I certainly shall not. Your sisters are engaged, and there is not another woman in the room whom it would not be a punishment to dance with."

"I would not be as particular as you are," cried Bingley.

"*You* are dancing with the only handsome girl," said Darcy, looking at the eldest Miss Bennet.

"Oh! she is the most beautiful creature I ever saw! But there is one of her sisters siting down just behind you, who is very pretty, and I dare say very agreeable."

"Which do you mean?" and turning round, he looked for a moment at Elizabeth and coldly said, "She is not handsome enough to tempt *me*."

Mr Darcy walked off and Elizabeth remained with no very friendly feeling towards him. The evening passed off pleasantly. Mrs Bennet had seen her eldest daughter much admired by the Netherfield party. Mr Bingley had danced with her twice. Jane was as much pleased by this, though in a quieter way. Elizabeth felt Jane's pleasure.

---

turned the tide of his popularity: turned people's opinion against him

Mary had heard herself mentioned to Miss Bingley as the most accomplished girl in the neighbourhood; and Catherine and Lydia had been fortunate enough to be never without a partner, which was all they cared for at a party.

They returned in good spirits to Longbourn, the village where they lived, and of which they were the principal inhabitants. They found Mr Bennet up, reading a book. Mrs Bennet poured out a long description of the number of dances Mr Bingley had danced and all his partners. She talked till her husband impatiently stopped her, saying he wished Mr Bingley had broken his ankle in the first dance.

When Jane and Elizabeth were alone, Jane told her sister how very much she admired Mr Bingley.

"He is sensible, good-humoured, lively, and I never saw such pleasant manners! So much ease and such politeness. I was much pleased that he asked me to dance a second time. I did not expect such a compliment."

"That is one great difference between us. Compliments and praise always take *you* by surprise, and *me* never," said Elizabeth. "You were about five times as pretty as any other woman in the room. However, he certainly is very agreeable and I give you leave to like him. But you never see a fault in anybody. And so you like this man's sisters too, do you? Their manners are not like his."

"Not at first, but they are very pleasing women."

Elizabeth did not believe this. They were, in fact, fine ladies, but proud and conceited; and were agreeable only when they chose to be so. Mr Bingley had inherited property to the amount of nearly a hundred thousand pounds from his father and was now planning to buy an estate of his own.

Between him and Darcy there was a very close and steady friendship in spite of great differences in character. Darcy was drawn to Bingley by the easiness, frankness, and sweetness of temper. Bingley had great faith in Darcy's judgement. In understanding, Darcy was superior, though Bingley was by no means wanting in it. Darcy was at the same time haughty, reserved and too particular; and his manners, though well-bred, were not pleasant. Bingley was sure of being liked wherever he appeared; Darcy was always giving offence.

Within a short distance of Longbourn lived a family with whom the Bennets were very friendly. Sir William Lucas had been in trade, but had made a small fortune and risen to the honour of knighthood. Though proud of his rank he was friendly and obliging. Lady Lucas was a very good kind of woman, not too clever to be a valuable neighbour to Mrs Bennet. They had several children. The eldest of them, a sensible, intelligent young woman of about twenty-seven, was Elizabeth's good friend. It was but natural that the Miss Lucases and the Miss Bennets should meet to talk over a ball was absolutely necessary; so the morning saw the former coming over to Longbourn.

The ladies of Longbourn soon called upon those of Netherfield, and the visit was returned, as was the custom. Miss Bennet's pleasing manners won the good opinion of Mrs Hurst and Miss Bingley. Their mother was found to be unbearable and the younger sisters not worth speaking to, but they wished to know the eldest better. Jane was very pleased but Elizabeth saw through their pride even in their manner towards her sister, and could not like them. It was clear that their brother *did* admire Jane and it was equally clear to Elizabeth that Jane was on the way to being very much in love. But this was not likely to be discovered by the world, as Jane combined strong feeling with a composed and cheerful manner.

Indeed Charlotte sounded a note of warning to Elizabeth on this point. "It is sometimes a disadvantage to be so guarded.

---

in trade: employed in business, in buying and selling goods
knighthood: a title conferred on a man by the king or queen of England that enables him to carry the title Sir before his name

Bingley likes your sister, undoubtedly, but he may never do more than like her, if she does not help him on."

While Elizabeth was thus observing Mr Bingley's attention to her sister, she did not suspect that she was herself becoming an object of some interest in the eyes of his friend. Mr Darcy had at first scarcely allowed her to be pretty. But no sooner had he decided that she had hardly a good feature in her face, than he began to find that it was made uncommonly intelligent by the beautiful expression of her dark eyes. He also noticed that her figure was graceful and pleasing and he was attracted by her lively, playful manner. But to Elizabeth he was only the man who made himself agreeable nowhere, and had not thought her handsome enough to dance with.

He began to wish to know her better, and presently an opportunity arose. One day at Sir William Lucas's where some ladies were dancing with some officers, Mr Darcy stood silent and unapproachable. Sir William began to talk, but Mr Darcy said very little. They saw Elizabeth at the moment moving towards them, and Sir William called out to her.

"My dear Miss Eliza, why are you not dancing? Mr Darcy, you must allow me to present this young lady to you as a very desirable partner," and taking her hand, he would have given it to Mr Darcy, who, though very surprised, was willing to take it, when she instantly drew back.

"Indeed, sir, I have not the least intention of dancing. I sincerely hope that you do not suppose I came this way to beg for a partner."

Mr Darcy with great politeness asked for the honour of the dance, but in vain. Nor did Sir William succeed in changing her mind by his attempt at persuasion.

"Mr Darcy is all politeness," said Elizabeth, smiling, and turned away. Her resistance had not spoilt Mr Darcy's idea about her, and he still thought of her with some pleasure, when Miss Bingley spoke to him.

"You are considering how difficult it would be to pass many evenings in this company."

"Your guess is wrong. I have been meditating on the very great pleasure which a pair of fine eyes in the face of a pretty woman can bestow."

Miss Bingley immediately asked for the name of the lady with such fine eyes.

"Miss Elizabeth Bennet."

"Is she such a great favourite? Then I shall consider the matter as absolutely settled. You will have a charming mother-in-law," cried Miss Bingley. Mr Darcy listened with perfect indifference, and his composure made her feel that all was safe.

---

meditating: thinking long and carefully

3

Jane Gets an Invitation

Mr Bennet's property consisted almost entirely of an estate of two thousand a year. Unfortunately for his daughters, this was entailed. In the absence of male heirs the property would pass to a distant relation; and their mother's fortune could not make up for a shortage in his income. Mrs Bennet had a sister in Meryton, married to a Mr Philips, and a brother settled in London.

The village of Longbourn was only one mile from Meryton. The two youngest of the family, Catherine and Lydia, often walked to Meryton to visit their aunt, stopping at a milliner's shop just over the way. At present they were well supplied with news and happiness. A regiment had recently arrived in the neighbourhood and was to remain for the whole winter. They could talk of nothing but the officers.

After listening one morning to their remarks on the subject Mr Bennet coolly observed, "You must be two of the silliest girls in the country."

"I am astonished, my dear," said Mrs Bennet, "that you should be so ready to think your own children silly. As it happens they are all very clever."

---

entailed: law by which only male heirs, even if only distantly related, inherit the property of a man, and the owner may not sell or give away the property

Catherine was upset at her father's remark, but Lydia was quite undisturbed, and continued to chatter about the officers. Just then a servant came with a note for Miss Bennet from Netherfield. Mrs Bennet's eyes sparkled with pleasure and she was eagerly calling out while her daughter read it.

"It is from Miss Bingley," said Jane. "She invites me to dine with herself and Mrs Hurst. The gentlemen are to dine with the officers."

"Dining out," said Mrs Bennet; "that is very unlucky."

"Can I have the carriage?" said Jane.

"No, my dear, you had better go on horseback, because it seems likely to rain; and then you must stay all night."

"I had much rather go in the carriage."

"But my dear, your father cannot spare the horses; they are wanted in the farm."

Jane had therefore to go on horseback. Her mother followed her to the door, hoping cheerfully for bad weather. Soon after Jane had left it rained hard. Her sisters were uneasy for her but her mother was delighted. The rain continued the whole evening without stopping. Jane certainly could not come back. Breakfast was scarcely over next morning when a servant from Netherfield brought a note for Elizabeth from Jane saying that she was ill, with a headache and sore throat.

"Well, my dear," said Mr Bennet, "if your daughter should die, it would be a comfort to know that it was all done to attract Mr Bingley under your orders."

"People do not die of trifling colds," said Mrs Bennet. "As long as she stays there, it is all very well."

Elizabeth was really anxious and determined to see her sister. The carriage was not available and she was no horsewoman, so she decided to walk.

"How can you be so silly?" cried her mother. "Walk in all this mud? You will not be fit to be seen when you get there."

"I shall be fit to see Jane—which is all I want."

Catherine and Lydia accompanied her to Meryton, and then Elizabeth continued her walk alone. She quickly crossed field after field and found herself at last within view of the house, with tired ankles, dirty stockings, and a face rosy with the warmth of exercise.

Her appearance caused a great deal of surprise. Elizabeth felt that Miss Bingley and Mrs Hurst looked down on her for walking three miles in such bad weather. She was received, however, very politely by them; and in their brother's manners there was something more than politeness, there was good humour and kindness. Mr Darcy said very little. He was admiring the colour which exercise had given to her face.

Her sister had slept badly, was feverish and not well enough to leave her room. The doctor came, advised her to stay in bed and promised to send some medicine. At three o'clock Elizabeth felt she must go. But Jane showed such concern at parting with her that Miss Bingley could do nothing but invite her to remain at Netherfield for the present, and Elizabeth most thankfully agreed.

At half past six Elizabeth was called down to dinner. Jane was by no means better. Mr Bingley's sisters, on hearing this, repeated how sorry they were, how much they disliked being ill themselves, and then thought no more of the matter.

Their brother's concern for Jane was, however, very clear and his attention to Elizabeth prevented her feeling unwelcome. When dinner was over she returned at once to Jane, and Miss Bingley began to ridicule her as soon as she was out of the room; her manners were very bad indeed, she could not talk, had no taste and no beauty.

"I thought Miss Elizabeth Bennet looked remarkably well when she came into the room. It shows an affection for her sister which is very pleasing," said Bingley.

"I am afraid, Mr Darcy," said Miss Bingley in a half whisper, "that this experience has rather spoilt your admiration for her fine eyes."

"Not at all," he replied, "they were brightened by the exercise."

"I have the greatest affection for Jane Bennet," began Mrs Hurst, "she is really a very sweet girl, and I wish with all my heart she was well settled. But with such a mother and father, and such low relations, I am afraid there is no chance of it."

"It must certainly lessen her chance of marrying a man of any importance," Darcy remarked. To this speech Bingley made no answer, but his sisters heartily agreed, and made jokes about their friend's poor relations.

Elizabeth passed most of the night in her sister's room and in the morning asked to have a note sent to Longbourn asking her mother to visit Jane and form her own judgement of her condition. The note was immediately sent. Mrs Bennet, accompanied by her two youngest girls, reached Netherfield soon after the family breakfast. Being satisfied after seeing her that Jane's illness was not alarming, Mrs Bennet had no wish for her rapid recovery. Bingley met Mrs Bennet with hopes that she had not found her daughter worse.

"Indeed I have, sir," was her answer. "She is a great deal too ill to be moved."

"Removed!" cried Bingley. "It must not be thought of!"

When Mr Bingley expressed his concern about her daughter's health, Mrs Bennet thanked him for his kindness to Jane and added an apology for troubling him also with Lizzy. Mr Bingley was sincerely polite in his answer and forced his younger sister to say whatever was necessary. She spoke without much warmth, but Mrs Bennet was easily satisfied.

In the evening Elizabeth joined the party in the drawing room, where Mr Darcy was writing a letter. When his letter was written, he requested Miss Bingley and Elizabeth for some music. Miss Bingley moved eagerly to the piano and Mrs Hurst sang with her sister. While they were singing, Elizabeth could not help observing how frequently Mr Darcy's eyes were fixed on her. She could hardly suppose the she was an object of admiration to so great a man; and yet that he should look at her because he disliked her was still more strange. But she liked him too little to care how he felt.

When Miss Bingley started a lively Scotch tune, Mr Darcy said to Elizabeth.

"Wouldn't you desire to take this opportunity to dance a reel?"

She smiled but didn't answer. Surprised at her silence, he repeated the question.

"Oh!" said she, "I heard you before, but I could not immediately decide what to say in reply. You wanted me to say 'yes' so that you might have the pleasure of despising my taste, but I always delight in overthrowing these schemes. I have, therefore, made up my mind to tell you that I do not want to dance a reel at all, and now despise me if you dare."

"Indeed, I do not dare."

Elizabeth, having expected to annoy him, was greatly surprised at his courtesy. There was a mixture of sweetness and charm in her manner which made it difficult for her to displease anybody, and Darcy had never been so attracted by any woman as he was by her. He really believed that but for her inferior social position, he would be in some danger of falling in love with her. Miss Bingley saw enough to be jealous and was all the more anxious to get rid of Elizabeth.

Jane was well enough to leave her room that evening, and Elizabeth brought her down to the drawing room where she was welcomed by her two friends. Elizabeth noticed with great delight that Bingley seemed very happy to see her.

---

reel: a lively Scottish dance

Elizabeth wrote next morning to her mother begging that the carriage might be sent for them in the course of the day. Mrs Bennet sent word that they could not possibly have it before Tuesday. But Elizabeth was determined not to stay longer, so she urged Jane to borrow Mr Bingley's carriage immediately.

The master of the house tried to persuade Jane that she was not well enough to travel, but Jane was firm.

They were not welcomed home very warmly by their mother, who wanted them to stay at Netherfield as long as possible. But their father was really glad to see them.

4

A LETTER FROM MR COLLINS

"I hope, my dear," said Mr Bennet to his wife next morning, "that you have ordered a good dinner today, because I have reason to expect an addition to our family party."

"Who do you mean, my dear? I know of nobody that is coming, I am sure, unless Charlotte Lucas should happen to call—and I hope *my* dinners are good enough for her."

"The person of whom I speak is a gentleman and a stranger."

Mrs Bennet's eyes sparkled, "It is Mr Bingley, I am sure. Why, Jane—you never dropped a word of this, you sly thing!

"It is *not* Mr Bingley," said her husband; "it is a person whom I never saw in my life."

Everyone was astonished. Mr Bennet explained: "About a month ago, I received a letter from my cousin, Mr Collins, who, when I am dead, may turn you all out of this house as soon as he pleases."

"Oh! my dear," cried his wife, "I cannot bear to hear that mentioned. If I had been you, I should have tried long ago to do something or other about it."

Jane and Elizabeth had attempted to explain to her the nature of an entail. But it was a subject on which she was beyond the reach of reason.

"But if you will listen to this letter, you may perhaps be a little softened by his manner," replied Mr Bennet.

Hunsford, near Westerham, Kent,
15th October

Dear Sir,

The disagreement between yourself and my late honoured father always gave me much uneasiness, and since I have had the misfortune to lose him. I have frequently wished to end the quarrel. Having received ordination at Easter, I have been so fortunate as to receive the patronage of the Right Honourable Lady Catherine de Bourgh, widow of Sir Lewis de Bourgh, who most generously has assigned to me this valuable parish where I will most earnestly try to carry out all my duties. As a clergyman I feel it my duty to spread the blessings of peace in all families around me. On these grounds I flatter myself that my present offer of goodwill is praiseworthy and that the fact of my being next in the entail of Longbourn Estate will kindly be overlooked by you and you will not reject the offered olive branch. I am unhappy at being the means of injuring your fair daughters. I beg your pardon for it and promise to do all I can to make up for it. If you have no objection to receiving me in your house I shall have the pleasure of visiting you and your family on Monday, November 18th at four o'clock and shall probably stay till Saturday.

I remain, dear sir, with respectful compliments to your wife and daughters, your well-wisher and friend,

William Collins

---

ordination: ceremony of being appointed as a priest
patronage: support or encouragement given by a person
parish: small division of a country with its own priest and church (the chief landowner of an area often had the power to appoint priests for the local church)
offered olive branch: offer of peace

Mr Collins came punctually at four o'clock. His letter was pompous but his intention was kind, so he was received with great politeness by the whole family. Mr Bennet said little but the ladies were ready to talk and so was Mr Collins. He was tall, heavy-looking, and about twenty-five years of age. His manners were serious and formal. He complimented Mrs Bennet on having so fine a family of daughters and added that he did not doubt her seeing them all soon happily married.

"You are very kind, sir. I wish with all my heart it may prove so; otherwise they will be penniless. Things are arranged in such a strange manner. Not that I mean to find fault with you."

"I am aware, madam, of the hardship to my fair cousins. But I can tell them that I come prepared to admire them. At present I will not say much, but perhaps when we know each other better—"

He was interrupted by a call to dinner and the girls smiled at each other. The dinner was much praised, and Mr Collins asked which of his fair cousins was responsible for the cooking. This displeased Mrs Bennet, who assured him that they were very well able to keep a good cook, and her daughters had nothing to do in the kitchen.

Mr Collins was not a sensible man but a rather odd mixture of pride, self-importance and humility. Having now a good house and a sufficient income, he intended to marry. In seeking to be friendly with the Longbourn family he had a wife in view, as he meant to choose one of the daughters. This was his plan to make up to them for inheriting their father's estate and he thought it an excellent one and very generous on his part.

His plan did not vary on seeing them. Jane's lovely face charmed him; and for the first evening she was his settled choice. The next morning, however, he made an alteration, for

---

pompous: full of a sense of his own importance

Mrs Bennet smilingly warned him, "As to my *younger* daughters I could not positively answer, but my *eldest* daughter—I must just mention—is likely to be very soon engaged." Mr Collins had only to change from Jane to Elizabeth and it was soon done.

Mrs Bennet hoped that she might soon have two daughters married; and she was now highly pleased with the man whom she could not bear to speak of yesterday. Lydia had decided to walk to Meryton and all the sisters except Mary agreed to go with her. Mr Collins was to accompany them at the request of Mr Bennet, who was most anxious to get rid of him and have the library to himself.

On entering Meryton, the attention of every lady was soon caught by a young man of most gentleman-like appearance, walking with an officer, Mr Denny, whom Lydia and Kitty knew. Mr Denny introduced his friend, Mr Wickham, who he was happy to say had just joined the regiment. The young man needed only a uniform to make him completely charming to the ladies. He had a handsome face, a good figure and very pleasing manners. The whole party was standing and talking together very agreeably when the sound of horses drew their notice and Darcy and Bingley were seen riding down the street.

The two gentlemen came towards them and greeted them politely. Mr Bingley was then, he said, on his way to Longbourn to inquire after Jane. Mr Darcy bowed and was beginning to decide not to fix his eyes on Elizabeth, when he suddenly noticed the stranger. Elizabeth happening to see the faces of both as they looked at each other, was astonished. Both changed colour; one looked white, the other red. Mr Wickham, after a few moments, touched his hat—a greeting which Mr Darcy returned very slightly. What could be the meaning of this? It was impossible to imagine and it was also impossible not to want to know.

In another minute, Mr Bingley took leave and rode on with his friend, and the sisters went on to their aunt, Mrs Philips. Some of the officers were to dine with the Philipses the next day, and their aunt promised her nieces to make her husband invite Mr Wickham, if the family from Longbourn would come in the evening.

The carriage took Mr Collins and his five cousins at a suitable hour to Meryton, and the girls were happy to hear as they entered the drawing room, that Mr Wickham had accepted their uncle's invitation.

Mr Wickham was the happy man towards whom almost every female eye was turned, and Elizabeth the happy woman by whom he finally seated himself. The agreeable manner in which he immediately fell into conversation made her feel that the commonest topics would be made interesting by the skill of the speaker. What she chiefly wished to hear was the history of his acquaintance with Mr Darcy. Mr Wickham began the subject himself by inquiring in a hesitating manner how long Mr Darcy had been staying at Netherfield.

"About a month," said Elizabeth and then, unwilling to let the subject drop, added. "He is a man of very large property in Derbyshire, I understand."

"Yes," replied Wickham, "and his estate there is a noble one. A clear ten thousand a year. You could not have met a person more capable of giving you information on that head than myself—for I have been connected with his family from childhood."

Elizabeth could not but look surprised.

"You may well be surprised, Miss Bennet, to hear this, after seeing the very cold manner of our meeting yesterday. Are you well acquainted with Mr Darcy?"

"As much as I ever wish to be," cried Elizabeth warmly. "I think him very disagreeable."

"I wonder," said Wickham, "whether he is likely to be in this part of the country much longer."

"I do not at all know. I hope your plans will not be affected by his being in the neighbourhood."

"Oh, no!—we are not on friendly terms, but I have no reason for avoiding *him*; if *he* wishes to avoid seeing *me*, he must go. His father was one of the best men that ever breathed, the truest friend I ever had. I could forgive Mr Darcy anything and everything rather than his disappointing the hopes and disgracing the memory of his father."

Elizabeth's interest in the subject increased, but delicacy prevented further questions.

"A military life is not what I was intended for. I was brought up for the church and I should at this time have been in possession of a most valuable living, had it pleased Mr Darcy. The late Mr Darcy, the father of the present Mr Darcy, and my godfather, in his will left me the best living he could provide, when it fell vacant. But this living was given elsewhere."

"Good heavens!" cried Elizabeth. "How could the will be disregarded? Why did you not take any legal steps?"

"The will was so worded as to give me no hope from law. A man of honour could not have doubted the intention, but Mr Darcy chose to treat it as a conditional recommendation. He stated that I had lost all claims to it by extravagance and imprudence. I have a warm unguarded temper, and I may

---

delicacy: sensitiveness, consideration for others' feelings

living: the church and the property going with it, including a house, given into the care of a clergyman by his patron, in return for preaching and other duties in the parish

godfather: a man who at baptism promises to look after a child's religious education

extravagance: wastefulness

imprudence: rashness

perhaps have sometimes spoken my opinion of him and to him too freely. But the fact is that he hates me."

"This is shocking! He deserves to be publicly disgraced."

"Some time or other he *will* be, but it will not be by *me*. Till I can forget his father I can never defy or expose him."

Elizabeth honoured him for such feelings, and exclaimed, "To treat in such a manner, the godson, the friend, the favourite of his father!"

"We were born in the same parish; and the greatest part of our youth was passed together. My father devoted all his time to the care of Pemberley property."

"How strange!" cried Elizabeth, "I wonder that the very pride of Mr Darcy has not made him just to you!"

"It *is* wonderful"—replied Wickham—"for almost all his actions may be traced to pride. It has often led him to be generous—to assist his tenants, and give relief to the poor. He has also *brotherly* pride, which with *some* brotherly affection, makes him a very kind and careful guardian of his sister."

"What sort of a girl is Miss Darcy?"

"I wish I could call her agreeable. It gives me pain to speak ill of a Darcy. But she is too much like her brother—very, very proud."

After many pauses Elizabeth began again.

"I am astonished at his friendship with Mr Bingley. How can Mr Bingley, who seems to be sweet-tempered and amiable, be friendly with such a man?"

"Mr Darcy can please when he chooses. Among those whom he considers his social equals, he is a very different man from what he is to the less prosperous."

Just then Mr Collins mentioned Lady Catherine de Bourgh. Mr Wickham, after observing Mr Collins for a few minutes,

---

amiable: friendly

asked Elizabeth whether her relation was very friendly with the family of de Bourgh.

"Lady Catherine de Bourgh," she replied, "has lately given him the living."

"You know of course that Lady Catherine de Bourgh and Lady Anne Darcy were sisters. Her daughter, Miss de Bourgh, will have a very large fortune, and it is believed that she and her cousin Mr Darcy will unite the two estates."

This information made Elizabeth smile as she thought of poor Miss Bingley. Vain indeed must be all her attentions if he was already promised to another.

5

The Ball at Netherfield

Elizabeth told Jane the next day what had passed between Mr Wickham and herself. Jane listened with astonishment and concern—she did not know how to believe that Mr Darcy could be so unworthy of Mr Bingley's regard. Jane could never believe ill of anybody. "They have both been deceived, I dare say, in some way of which we can form no idea."

Just then Mr Bingley and his sisters came to give their personal invitation for the long expected ball at Netherfield, which was fixed for the following Tuesday. The prospect of the ball was extremely agreeably to all the girls. Elizabeth's spirits were so high that she could not help asking Mr Collins whether he intended to join in the evening's amusements and she was rather surprised when he said, "I am so far from objecting to dancing myself that I shall hope to be honoured with the hands of all my fair cousins in the course of the evening; and I take this opportunity of requesting yours, Miss Elizabeth, for the two first dances especially."

Elizabeth had expected to be engaged by Mr Wickham for these very dances—and to have Mr Collins instead! There was no help for it, however, and the proposal had to be accepted. It now first struck her that *she* was selected from among her sisters as worthy of being the mistress of Hunsford Parsonage.

---

parsonage: the house provided for the parson or priest

The idea was confirmed as she observed his frequent attempts at a compliment on her wit and liveliness. It was not long before her mother gave her to understand that such a marriage was exceedingly agreeable to her. Elizabeth however did not choose to take the hint, being well aware that her reply would result in a serious dispute. Mr Collins might never make the offer; and till he did, it was useless to quarrel about him.

Till Elizabeth entered the drawing room at Netherfield and looked in vain for Mr Wickham, any doubt of his being present had never occurred to her. But in an instant arose the dreadful suspicion of his being purposely omitted for Mr Darcy's pleasure in the Bingleys' invitation to the officers. However, his friend, Mr Denny, told them that Wickham had to go to town on business, and added,

"I do not imagine his business would have called him away just now, if he had not wished to avoid a certain gentleman here."

Every feeling of displeasure against Mr Darcy was so sharpened by immediate disappointment that she could hardly reply when Mr Darcy approached her a little later. The first two dances were dances which caused her great annoyance, for Mr Collins was very awkward.

When those dances were over, so suddenly did Mr Darcy surprise her by his request for a dance that she accepted him without knowing what she did. She soon noticed that everybody seemed surprised at the honour done to her by being asked to dance with him. For some time they did not speak a single word. Later he asked her if she and her sisters often walked to Meryton. Unable to resist the temptation she said, "When you met us there the other day, we had just been forming a new acquaintance."

The effect was immediate. A deeper shade of haughtiness spread over his face, but he did not say a word. At length he said,

"Mr Wickham has such pleasant manners that he can always make friends—whether he may be equally capable of retaining them, is less certain."

"He has been so unlucky as to lose *your* friendship," replied Elizabeth, "and in a manner which he is likely to suffer from all his life."

At that moment Sir William stopped with a bow to compliment Mr Darcy on his dancing and his partner.

"I have been most pleased, indeed, my dear sir. Such superior dancing is not often seen. I hope to have this pleasure often repeated, especially when a certain desirable event, my dear Miss Eliza"—glancing at her sister and Bingley—"will take place."

Sir William's reference to his friend seemed to strike Mr Darcy forcibly, and his eyes were directed with a very serious expression towards Bingley and Jane, who were dancing together.

Soon afterwards Elizabeth exclaimed, "I remember hearing you once say, Mr Darcy, that you hardly ever forgave, that your anger once aroused was difficult to calm. You are very careful, I suppose, about starting it, and never allow yourself to be blinded by prejudice?"

"I hope not," replied Darcy. "May I ask why you question thus?"

She shook her head. "I hear such different accounts of you as puzzle me exceedingly."

They had not long separated when Miss Bingley came and addressed her,

"So, Miss Eliza, I hear that you are quite delighted with George Wickham. Your sister has been asking me a thousand questions about him. I find that the young man forgot to tell

---

prejudice: opinion, usually dislike, formed before sufficient knowledge or experience of the matter

you that his father was the late Mr Darcy's steward. Let me remind you, however, as a friend, not to have perfect faith in what he says. As to Mr Darcy's treating him badly, it is perfectly false; on the contrary, he has been always remarkably kind to him, though Wickham has treated him shamefully. I know very well that Mr Darcy is not in the least to blame, but really, considering Wickham's family, one could not expect much better."

"His guilt and his descent appear by your account to be the same," said Elizabeth angrily; "for I have heard you accuse him of nothing worse than of being the son of Mr Darcy's steward, and of *that*, I can assure you, he informed me himself."

Miss Bingley, turning away with a sneer, said, "Excuse my interference. It was kindly meant."

Elizabeth then sought her eldest sister, who had undertaken to make inquiries on the same subject from Bingley.

"I have nothing satisfactory to tell you," said Jane. "Mr Bingley is quite ignorant of the circumstances which have offended Mr Darcy; but he will answer for the good conduct and honour of his friend. Mr Wickham is by no means a respectable young man and has deserved to lose Mr Darcy's regard."

"I have not a doubt of Mr Bingley's sincerity," said Elizabeth warmly. "But since he is unacquainted with several parts of the story and has learnt the rest from that friend himself, I shall think of both the gentlemen as I did before."

When they sat down to supper she was deeply annoyed to find that her mother was talking to Lady Lucas, freely, openly and of nothing else but of her expectation that Jane would be soon married to Mr Bingley.

---

steward: someone who manages the property of another (usually large property)

descent: family and ancestry

In vain did Elizabeth try to check the rapidity of her mother's words or persuade her to describe her joy in a less audible whisper for she could see that it was overheard by Mr Darcy. The expression on his face changed gradually from contempt to steady gravity. The rest of the evening brought Elizabeth little amusement.

---

audible: loud enough to be heard

6

A pompous proposal

The next day opened a new scene at Longbourn. On finding Mrs Bennet, Elizabeth and one of the younger girls together, soon after breakfast, Mr Collins said to her, "May I hope, madam, for the honour of a private audience with your fair daughter Elizabeth?"

"Oh, dear! Yes—certainly," Mrs Bennet answered. "I am sure Lizzy will be happy. Come Kitty, I want you upstairs." She was hastening away when Elizabeth called out, "Dear ma'am, do not go. Mr Collins can have nothing to say to me that anybody need not hear. I am going away myself."

"No, no, nonsense, Lizzy. I *insist* you will stay where you are."

A moment's thought made Elizabeth feel that it would be wisest to get it over as soon as and as quietly as possible. As soon as Mrs Bennet and Kitty had gone Mr Collins began.

"Believe me, my dear Miss Elizabeth, that your modesty adds to your other perfections. You would have been less attractive in my eyes had there *not* been this little unwillingness. Almost as soon as I entered the house, I singled you out as the companion of my future life. But before I let my feelings run away with me on the subject it would be advisable to state my reasons for marrying—and moreover for coming into Hertfordshire with the design of selecting a wife, as I certainly did."

As he continued, the idea of Mr Collins with all his serious composure being run away with by his feelings made Elizabeth smile.

"First, I think it a right thing for every clergyman to set the example of marriage in his parish. Secondly, I am sure it will add very greatly to my happiness; and thirdly, I have been advised to marry by the very noble lady who is my patroness. And, my fair cousin, I must add that the notice and kindness of Lady Catherine de Bourgh is not among the least of the advantages I can offer you."

"Since I am to inherit this estate after the death of your father, I wished to choose a wife from amongst his daughters, so that the loss to him would be as little as possible. Now nothing more remains except to assure you of the greatness of my love. To fortune I am perfectly indifferent, and shall make no demand on your father, since I know that it could not be complied with."

It was absolutely necessary to interrupt him now.

"You are too hasty sir," Elizabeth cried "You forget that I have made no answer. Accept my thanks for the compliment you are paying me, but it is impossible for me to do otherwise than decline your proposal."

"I believe," replied Mr Collins with a wave of his hand, "that it is usual with young ladies to refuse the proposal of the man whom they secretly mean to accept, when he first applies for their favour. I am not discouraged, and shall hope to lead you to the altar ere long."

"I do assure you," cried Elizabeth, "that I am not one of these young ladies, who dare to risk their happiness on the chance of being asked a second time. You could not make me happy and

---

to fortune, I am perfectly indifferent: I have no interest in getting a wife with a dowry

to lead you to the altar: to marry you

I am sure that I am the last woman in the world who would make you so."

"You must give me leave to flatter myself my dear cousin, that your refusal of my offer is merely a form of words. I do not believe my hand is unworthy of your acceptance. My situation in life, my connections with the family of a de Bourgh, are all highly in my favour; and in spite of your many attractions, the portion of money which you inherit is so small that you may not receive many other offers of marriage."

"I thank you again for the honour you have done me, but to accept is absolutely impossible."

"I am sure that, when sanctioned by both your parents, my proposal will not fail to be accepted by you."

To such continued self-deception Elizabeth would make no reply, and immediately and in silence withdrew, determined that if he persisted, she would appeal to her father, whose negative would be expressed in a more decisive manner.

Mr Collins was not left alone long, for Mrs Bennet entered the breakfast room and congratulated both him and herself. Mr Collins received and returned the good wishes with equal pleasure and then told her the details of their conversation.

This information, however, startled Mrs Bennet.

"Lizzy is a headstrong, foolish girl and does not know her own interest. But I will *make* her know it," she said.

So far Mr Collins had believed that his cousin's refusal was due only to her bashful modesty. But on hearing Mrs Bennet he said, "If she is really so headstrong and foolish, she wouldn't be a very desirable wife to a man in my situation."

This alarmed Mrs Bennet, and she hurried to her husband, calling out as she entered the library.

"Oh! Mr Bennet, you are wanted immediately. You must come and make Lizzy marry Mr Collins for she vows that she

headstrong: obstinate
bashful: shy

will not have him and if you do not make haste *he* will not have *her*."

Mr Bennet raised his eyes from his book and fixed them on her face with a calm unconcern.

"I have not the pleasure of understanding you," said he. "Of what are you talking?"

"Lizzy declares she will not have Mr Collins, and Mr Collins begins to say that he will not have Lizzy."

"And what am I to do on the occasion? It seems a hopeless business."

"Speak to Lizzy about it yourself. Tell her you insist upon her marrying him."

"Let her be called down. She will hear my opinion."

Elizabeth was summoned to the library.

"Come here, child," said her father. "I have sent for you on an affair of importance. I understand that Mr Collins has made you an offer of marriage. Is it true?" Elizabeth replied that it was. "Very well—and this offer of marriage you have refused?"

"I have, sir."

"Very well. We now come to the point. Your mother insists upon your accepting it. Is it not so, Mrs Bennet?"

"Yes, or I shall never see her again."

"An unhappy alternative is before you, Elizabeth. From this day you must be a stranger to one of your parents. Your mother will never see you again if you do *not* marry Mr Collins and I will never see you again if you *do*."

Elizabeth could not but smile at such a conclusion of such a beginning. However, in spite of her disappointment, Mrs Bennet did not give up the point. She coaxed and threatened Elizabeth by turns, but Elizabeth remained firm.

---

coaxed: tried to persuade her by getting her into a good temper first

Mr Collins meanwhile was quietly thinking over what had happened. He thought too well of himself to understand for what reason his cousin could refuse him.

Fortunately Charlotte Lucas came to spend the day with them. Mrs Bennet entreated her to persuade her friend, Lizzy, to comply with the wishes of all her family. She talked on till they were joined by Mr Collins, whereupon she declared that she wished to talk to him.

Elizabeth, Jane and Kitty left immediately. Charlotte was held up by Mr Collins's polite inquiries about her family. After these were replied to, she walked to the window and pretended not to hear, while Mr Collins stiffly informed Mrs Bennet that he was quite resigned to being rejected by Elizabeth and would withdraw his offer of marriage.

---

comply: act in accordance with

7

Charlotte's decision

Mr Collins's feelings were chiefly expressed, not by dejection, but by stiffness of manner and resentful silence. He scarcely ever spoke to Elizabeth. His attentions were transferred for the rest of the day to Miss Lucas, whose patience in listening to him was a relief to all. Elizabeth had hoped that his resentment might shorten his visit, but his plans did not appear to be affected by it.

After breakfast, the girls walked to Meryton to inquire if Mr Wickham had returned. He met them at their aunt's, where his regret and disappointment at missing the ball were talked over. To Elizabeth, however, he explained, "I found, as the time drew near, that I had better not meet Mr Darcy; to be in the same party with him would be more than I could bear."

Elizabeth highly approved of his behaviour. As Wickham and another officer walked back with the sisters to Longbourn, she felt that his accompanying them was a double advantage. It offered a compliment to herself and provided an opportunity to introduce him to her parents.

Soon after their return, a letter was delivered to Miss Bennet. It came from Netherfield. Elizabeth saw her sister's face change as she read it. Putting the letter away, Jane tried to join with her usual cheerfulness in the general conversation. But no sooner had the officers taken leave than a glance from Jane invited Elizabeth to follow her upstairs.

"This letter is from Caroline Bingley," Jane said, "What it contains has surprised me a great deal. The whole party has left Netherfield by this time, and are on their way to town, without any intention of coming back again." Though the suddenness of their departure surprised Elizabeth, she saw nothing in it really to be unhappy over. It was not to be supposed that their absence from Netherfield would prevent Mr Bingley's being there.

"I *will* read you the passage," Jane continued, "which particularly hurts me. 'Mr Darcy is impatient to see his sister. I really do not think Georgiana Darcy has her equal for beauty, grace or any other gifts. My brother admires her greatly; and with all these circumstances in favour of an attachment, we look forward to having her hereafter as our sister.'"

"Is it not clear enough," said Jane, "that Caroline is perfectly convinced that her brother does not care for me, and means (most kindly!) to put me on my guard?"

"Miss Bingley sees that her brother is in love with you," replied Elizabeth, "and wants him to marry Miss Darcy. She follows him to town hoping to keep him there, and tries to persuade you that he does not care about you."

"Caroline is incapable of wilfully deceiving anyone; and all that I can hope that she is deceiving herself."

"No one who has seen you together can doubt Mr Bingley's affection for you. But the case is this. We are not rich enough, or grand enough, for them. She is anxious to get Miss Darcy for her brother because she hopes that her own marriage to Mr Darcy will follow."

The idea of Mr Bingley's returning no more was treated by Elizabeth with such scorn that Jane was led to hope: believing that not only would he return to Netherfield, but answer every wish of her heart.

The Bennets were invited to dine with the Lucases, and during the greater part of the day Miss Lucas was so kind as to listen to Mr Collins.

"It keeps him in good humour and I am very grateful to you," said Elizabeth, and Charlotte told her that she was glad to be useful. But Elizabeth did not know that Charlotte's object was to attract Mr Collins herself. She was so successful that next morning Mr Collins hastened to Lucas Lodge to throw himself at her feet. In as short a time as his long speeches would allow, everything was settled between them to the satisfaction of both.

Sir William and Lady Lucas were speedily asked for their consent, which they gave joyfully. Mr Collins's present circumstances would make it a good marriage for their daughter, to whom they could give little fortune; and her husband would some day inherit Mr Bennet's property, which greatly improved his prospects.

Charlotte herself remained calm. She had gained her point. Mr Collins to be sure was neither sensible nor agreeable. But marriage had always been her object, because it was the only honourable provision for a well-educated young woman of small fortune, and she was already twenty-seven and not handsome either. Even if marriage might not bring happiness, it was a preservation from want.

She valued Elizabeth's friendship beyond that of any other person, and felt that Elizabeth would wonder and would probably blame her. So she decided to give her the information herself. She therefore made Mr Collins promise to drop no hint of what had happened. Next day she called soon after breakfast and told Elizabeth of the event. Elizabeth was so surprised that she could not help crying out.

"Engaged to Mr Collins! My dear Charlotte—impossible!"

"You must be very much surprised, as Mr Collins was wishing to marry you only a few days ago. But I am not romantic, you know. I only ask for a comfortable home; and considering Mr Collins's character, connections, situation in life, I feel that my chances of happiness are as fair as most people can expect." Elizabeth controlled herself and quietly wished her friend all happiness.

Sir William Lucas came over himself to announce his daughter's engagement. The treatment he received was not happy. Mrs Bennet refused to believe the story. She was sure that the two would never be happy together. Elizabeth and Jane, however, did their best to stop their mother. They spoke of Mr Collins's excellent character and the happiness that might be expected from such a match.

Elizabeth felt that there could be no confidence between her and Charlotte again. This made her turn with more fondness to her sister. Daily she was growing more anxious for Jane's happiness, as Bingley had now been gone a week and nothing was heard of his return. She began to fear—not that Bingley was indifferent—but that his sisters would be successful in keeping him away. As for Jane, she was most anxious to conceal the pain she felt; and even between herself and Elizabeth the subject was never raised. But an hour seldom passed in which Mrs Bennet did not talk with irritation of Netherfield and its master. It needed all Jane's steady mildness to bear this calmly.

---

confidence: trust

8

A CHANGE OF HEART

Miss Bingley's letter arrived in answer to one which Jane had sent earlier and put an end to doubt. The very first sentence made it clear that they had settled in London for the winter. The letter concluded with her brother's regret at not having had time to say goodbye to his friends before he left the county. Praise of Miss Darcy occupied the rest of the letter. Hope was entirely over. Elizabeth heard it all in silent anger at Bingley's easy temper and want of proper resolution. This had made it possible for his friends to sway him and led him to give up his own happiness according to their desires.

A day or two passed before Jane had the courage to speak of her feelings to Elizabeth.

"Oh! My dear mother can have no idea of the pain she gives me by her continued criticism of him. But I will not complain. He may live in my memory as the most amiable man I ever met, but that is all. In a little time, I shall try to get the better—"

"My dear Jane!" exclaimed Elizabeth, "you are too good. Your sweetness is angelic. *You* wish to think well of all the world, and are hurt if I speak ill of anybody."

"Beyond a doubt, his sisters wish him to choose Miss Darcy," Jane replied. "If they had believed him attached to me, they

sway: influence

would not have tried to part us; if he were so, they could not succeed. I am not, ashamed of having been mistaken. But I should not like to feel ill of him or his sisters. Let me take it in the best light."

Elizabeth could not oppose such a wish, and from this time Mr Bingley's name was scarcely ever mentioned between them.

Soon after, Mrs Bennet's brother and his wife came as usual to spend Christmas at Longbourn. Mr Gardiner was a sensible gentleman, very different from his sister. The Netherfield ladies would never have believed that a man living by trade could be so well-bred and agreeable. Mrs Gardiner was a pleasant, intelligent woman with graceful manners. She was a great favourite with her nieces, especially the two eldest, who often stayed with her in town.

As soon as Mrs Gardiner had distributed her presents and described the newest fashions, Mrs Bennet started to complain about her many disappointments. Two of her girls were on the point of getting married and in the end nothing had happened. Mrs Gardiner, who already knew something of this from her nieces' letters, turned the conversation.

When alone with Elizabeth afterwards, Mrs Gardiner said, "It seems likely to have been a desirable match for Jane. I am sorry it did not take place. With her character she may not get over it immediately. Do you think we could persuade her to go back to town with us? The change of scene might help."

Jane accepted her aunt's invitation with pleasure. The Gardiners stayed at Longbourn for a week. Mrs Gardiner, noticing Elizabeth's friendly behaviour towards Wickham, narrowly observed both of them. She decided to speak to Elizabeth on the subject before she left Hertfordshire.

Mrs Gardiner's warning to Elizabeth was given at the first favourable opportunity.

"Do not involve yourself, or try to involve him, in an affection which the want of fortune would make so very imprudent," she advised.

"He is the most agreeable man I ever saw," replied Elizabeth. "Yet I believe that it will be better if he does not become attached to me. I understand how unwise that would be. Oh! how abominable is Mr Darcy—but really, I will try to do what I think to be wisest."

Mr Collins returned to Hertfordshire soon after the Gardiners and Jane left. Thursday was to be the wedding day and on Wednesday Miss Lucas paid her farewell visit to the Bennets. When she rose to leave, Elizabeth, ashamed of her mother's ungracious behaviour, accompanied her out of the room. Charlotte said to her, "Promise me to come to Hunsford. My father and Maria are to come to me in March. Indeed, Eliza, you will be as welcome to me as either of them."

Elizabeth soon heard from her friend, and their correspondence was as regular and frequent as it had ever been. Charlotte wrote cheerfully of her home and neighbours and Lady Catherine's friendly behaviour.

Jane also wrote from London. She had been a week in town without seeing or hearing from Caroline. She explained it by supposing that her last letter to her friend had by some accident been lost. After paying them a visit, she wrote again. It seemed she had received a cool welcome.

Four weeks passed and Jane saw nothing of Mr Bingley. She tried to feel that she did not mind it. But she could no longer be blind to Miss Bingley's inattention. When at last the visitor did appear, the shortness of her stay, the unfriendliness of her manner would not allow Jane to deceive herself any longer. She wrote to Elizabeth, about it.

I confess to have been entirely deceived in Miss Bingley's regard for me. When she did come it was very evident that she had no pleasure in it. She made a formal apology for not calling before, and said not a word of wishing to see me again.

The letter gave Elizabeth some pain. She could see that Jane would no longer be deceived by the sister, and all expectation from the brother was now over. About herself, the information that she sent to Mrs Gardiner was such as might rather give contentment to her aunt than to herself. Wickham had given up his attentions to her, and was now the admirer of a young lady called Miss Mary King. The most remarkable charm of this young lady was that she had inherited a fortune of ten thousand pounds. However, Elizabeth's heart had been only slightly touched, and she did not grieve over the matter.

Elizabeth accompanied Sir William and his younger daughter on their visit to Charlotte. As they were to spend a night in London it would give her a chance to meet Jane also. As they drove to Mr Gardiner's door, Jane was there to welcome them. Elizabeth, looking into her face, was pleased to see it as healthy and lovely as ever. The day passed most pleasantly.

When Elizabeth sat by her aunt, their first subject was Jane. She was more grieved than astonished to hear that though Jane tried to be cheerful she was low spirited at times. Mrs Gardiner then spoke about Wickham's desertion, and said she was glad Elizabeth did not feel dejected, for in her opinion he seemed to be running after money.

Before they parted, Elizabeth had the unexpected happiness of an invitation to accompany her uncle and aunt on a tour of pleasure which they proposed to take during the summer. They had not quite decided where to go, but perhaps, to the Lakes. Nothing could have pleased Elizabeth more and she accepted gratefully.

Lakes: a district in north-west England, with beautiful mountains and lakes

9

A visit to Hunsford

Everything they saw in the next day's journey was new and interesting to Elizabeth, and she was in high spirits. Mr Collins and Charlotte were at the door of the parsonage. Mrs Collins welcomed her friend with the greatest pleasure. Elizabeth saw instantly that her cousin's manners were not altered by his marriage. His formal politeness was just what it had been.

She looked with wonder at her friend, that she could be so cheerful with such a companion. But when Mr Collins said something of which his wife might reasonably be ashamed, Charlotte wisely did not listen. Elizabeth learned that Lady Catherine was still in the country.

"Yes, Miss Elizabeth, you will have the honour of seeing her on the coming Sunday at church, and I need not say you will be delighted with her kindness and condescension."

"Lady Catherine is a very sensible woman indeed," said Charlotte, "and a most attentive neighbour."

"Very true, my dear," her husband added. "She is the sort of woman one cannot regard with too much respect."

In the solitude of her own room, Elizabeth wondered at Charlotte's contentment. She tried to understand the skill with which Charlotte guided her husband, and the composure with which she endured him, and had to admit that it was all done very well.

---

condescension: gracious behaviour showing feelings of superiority

The next day she heard a sudden noise and somebody running upstairs and calling loudly in great excitement. It was Charlotte's younger sister, Maria, a good-humoured but rather empty-headed girl.

"Oh, my dear Eliza, make haste and come down." When they ran down into the dining room in search of this wonder, it was two ladies in a carriage at the garden gate.

"And is this all?" cried Elizabeth. "I expected at least that the pigs had got into the garden, but it is only Lady Catherine and her daughter!"

Maria was shocked at the mistake. "It is not Lady Catherine. The old lady is Mrs Jenkinson, who lives with them, and the other is Miss de Bourgh. Only look at her. She is quite a little creature. Who could have thought that she could be so thin and small!"

"I like her appearance," said Elizabeth, remembering whom she was to marry. To herself she thought, "She looks sickly and cross. She will make him a very proper wife."

"She is abominably rude to keep Charlotte standing out of doors. Why doesn't she come in?" continued Elizabeth.

"Oh! Charlotte says she hardly ever does. It is the greatest of favours when Miss de Bourgh comes in."

At length the ladies drove away and Mr Collins congratulated the two girls on their good fortune. Charlotte explained this by telling them that the whole party was to dine next day at Rosings, the home of Lady Catherine.

Scarcely anything was talked of the whole day or next morning except their visit to Rosings. Mr Collins was carefully instructing them in what they were to expect, so that the sight of such rooms, so many servants and so splendid a dinner might not surprise them too much.

Her ladyship, rose to receive them. She was a tall, large woman, with strongly marked features. Her manner was not friendly or pleasant, nor such as to let her visitors forget their inferior rank. Whatever she said, was spoken in a commanding tone, so as to show her self-importance. Miss de Bourgh looked pale and sickly and spoke very little, except sometimes in a low voice to Mrs Jenkinson.

The dinner was very good, and there were all the servants and everything else which Mr Collins had described. Every dish was praised by him first and then by Sir William in such a manner that Elizabeth wondered how Lady Catherine could bear it. But she seemed satisfied by their excessive admiration and smiled most graciously.

When they returned to the drawing room, there was little to be done but hear Lady Catherine talk. She asked Elizabeth at different times how many sisters she had, whether they were older or younger than herself, whether any of them were likely to be married, whether they were pretty, where they had been educated, what carriage her father kept. Elizabeth could not help feeling how impolite she was, but answered composedly.

"Do you play and sing, Miss Bennet?" she asked.

"A little."

"Oh, then—some time or other we shall be happy to hear you. Our instrument is excellent, probably superior to—You shall try it someday. Do your sisters play and sing?"

"One of them does."

"Has your governess left you?"

"We never had any governess."

"No governess? Then who taught you?"

"Such of us as wished to learn never wanted the means. We were always encouraged to read and had all the masters that were necessary."

"Nothing is to be done in education without steady and regular instruction by a governess. Are any of your younger sisters out, Miss Bennet?"

Are any of your younger sisters out?: Have any of your younger sisters been introduced to society?

"Yes ma'am, all."

"All the younger sisters out before the older are married? Very odd!"

"But really, ma'am, I think it would be very hard upon the younger sisters if they could not have their share of amusement because the elders may not marry early."

"Upon my word," said her ladyship, "you give your opinion very decidedly for so young a person. Pray what is your age?"

"With three younger sisters grown up," replied Elizabeth, smiling, "Your Ladyship can hardly expect me to own it."

Lady Catherine was astonished at not receiving a direct answer.

Presently the card tables were brought in. When Lady Catherine and her daughter had played as long as they chose, the carriage was offered to Mrs Collins, gratefully accepted and immediately ordered.

10

An unexpected visitor

Sir William left after a week, but Elizabeth stayed on, and now saw more of her friend. The entertainment of dining at Rosings was repeated about twice a week. Elizabeth had heard that Mr Darcy was expected there. When he came he was accompanied by Colonel Fitzwilliam the younger son of Mr Darcy's uncle, Lord—as Mr Collins was careful to mention.

On the following morning Mr Collins hastened to Rosings to pay his respects and when he returned, to Charlotte's great surprise, the gentlemen accompanied him. Colonel Fitzwilliam was about thirty, not handsome, but in person and manners most truly a gentleman. Mr Darcy paid his compliments to Mrs Collins with his usual reserve. Elizabeth merely bowed to him without saying a word.

Colonel Fitzwilliam entered into conversation at once with the readiness and ease of a well-bred man, and talked very pleasantly. But his cousin sat for some time without speaking to anybody. At length his civility was so far awakened as to inquire after the health of Elizabeth's family. She answered him in the usual way and after a pause, added.

"My eldest sister has been in town these three months. Have you never happened to see her there?" She thought that he looked a little confused as he answered that he had never been so fortunate as to meet Miss Bennet. The subject was dropped and the gentlemen soon afterwards went away.

It was some days before the Collinses received another invitation to Rosings. Her ladyship, when there were visitors in the house, did not find their company necessary. On this occasion, they were not called for dinner, but merely asked to come to Rosings in the evening. Colonel Fitzwilliam however had called at the parsonage several times.

Colonel Fitzwilliam seemed really glad to see them. Mrs Collins's pretty friend had caught his fancy very much. He now seated himself by her and talked so agreeably that Elizabeth had never been so well entertained in the room before. They talked with so much spirit that they drew the attention of Lady Catherine herself, as well as of Mr Darcy. *His* eyes had been repeatedly turned towards them with a look of curiosity, and after a while her ladyship called out,

"What are you telling Miss Bennet? Let me hear what it is."

"We were speaking of music, madam," said he.

"Then pray speak aloud. There are few people in England, I suppose, who enjoy music more than myself or have a better natural taste. If I had ever learnt, I should have been very good at it. And so would Anne, if her health had allowed. How does Georgiana get on, Darcy?"

Mr Darcy spoke with affectionate praise of his sister's proficiency,

"I have told Miss Bennet several times, that she will never play really well, unless she practises more; and though Mrs Collins has no instrument, she is very welcome to play on the piano in Miss Jenkinson's room. She would be in nobody's way in that part of the house."

Mr Darcy looked a little ashamed of his aunt's ill-breeding and made no answer.

---

caught his fancy: pleased, attracted him
proficiency: ability to do something well and skillfully
ill-breeding: impolite behaviour

Presently Colonel Fitzwilliam reminded Elizabeth that she had promised to play for him. She sat down immediately, and he drew a chair near her. Lady Catherine listened to half a song and then talked as before to Mr Darcy, till he walked away and stood so as to get a full view of the fair performer's face. Elizabeth saw this and at the first convenient pause turned to him with an arch smile and said,

"You mean to frighten me, Mr Darcy, by coming in all this state to hear me though your sister *plays* so well. There is a stubbornness about me that never can bear to be frightened at the will of others. My courage always rises with every attempt to frighten me."

"You could not really believe that I had any intention of frightening you. I have had the pleasure of knowing you long enough to know that you find enjoyment at times in professing opinions which are in fact not your own."

Elizabeth laughed at this picture of herself. They were interrupted by Lady Catherine, who called out to know what they were talking about. Elizabeth immediately began playing again. Lady Catherine approached and said to Darcy,

"Miss Bennet would not play badly if she practised more. She has a very good notion of fingering though her taste is not equal to Anne's."

Elizabeth looked at Darcy to see how cordially he assented to his cousin's praise, but neither at that moment nor at any other could she discern any sign of love for his cousin.

Elizabeth was sitting by herself the next morning, writing to Jane, while Mrs Collins and Maria had gone to the village. She was startled by a ring at the door, and Mr Darcy entered the room alone. He seemed astonished too on finding her alone,

---

arch: mischievous
discern: see clearly

and apologised for his intrusion by saying that he understood that all the ladies were at home.

When her inquiries after Rosings were made, it seemed there would be total silence. So, feeling curious, she observed, "How very suddenly you all quitted Netherfield last November, Mr Darcy! I understand that Mr Bingley has not much idea of ever returning to Netherfield again."

"It is probable that he may spend very little of his time there in future. I should not be surprised," said Darcy, "if he were to give it up, as soon as anyone makes a satisfactory offer for the house."

Elizabeth made no answer. She was now determined to leave the trouble of finding a subject to him.

He took the hint, and soon began. "Mr Collins appears very fortunate in his choice of a wife."

"Yes, indeed; Mr Collins has met one of the few sensible women who would have accepted him, or have made him happy if they had. My friend has an excellent understanding and she seems perfectly happy. I am not sure that I consider her marrying Mr Collins the wisest thing she ever did, but it may certainly be called a good match for her in a prudential light."

Soon Charlotte and her sister returned from their walk. "What can be the meaning of this?" said Charlotte, as soon as he had gone. "My dear Eliza, he must be in love with you, or he would never have called on us in this familiar way."

But when Elizabeth told her of his silence it did not seem very likely, even to Charlotte's wishes, to be the case. The two cousins called at various times of the morning, sometimes separately, sometimes together. It was plain to them all that Colonel Fitzwilliam came because he had pleasure in their society. But why Mr Darcy came so often to the parsonage it was more

---

intrusion: entering without invitation
in a prudential light: from the point of view of care and forethought

difficult to understand. He seldom appeared really lively. Mrs Collins once or twice suggested the possibility of his being in love with her, but Elizabeth always laughed at the idea.

Elizabeth was re-reading Jane's last letter one day as she walked within the park when she looked up and saw that Colonel Fitzwilliam was approaching her.

"Do you definitely leave Kent on Saturday?" she asked.

"Yes—if Darcy does not put it off again. He likes to have his own way very well," replied Colonel Fitzwilliam.

"I imagine your cousin brought you down with him chiefly for the sake of having somebody at his disposal. I wonder he does not marry, to secure a lasting convenience of that kind. But perhaps his sister does as well for the present, and, as she is under his sole care, he may do what he likes with her."

"No," said Colonel Fitzwilliam. "I am joined with him in the guardianship of Miss Darcy."

"Are you indeed? Does your charge give you much trouble? Young ladies of her age are sometimes a little difficult to manage and if she has the true Darcy spirit, she may like to have her own way." As she spoke, she observed him looking at her earnestly. This convinced her that she had somehow or other got pretty near the truth. She continued directly.

"You need not be frightened, I never heard any harm of her; she is a great favourite with Mrs Hurst and Miss Bingley. I think I have heard you say that you know them."

"I know them a little. Their brother is a great friend of Darcy's."

"Oh! yes," said Elizabeth, "Mr Darcy is extremely kind to Mr Bingley and takes a great deal of care of him."

"Care of him! Yes, I really believe Darcy *does* take care of him in those points where he most wants care. From something

---

guardianship: position of someone who is legally responsible for the care of a young person and his property

that he told me in our journey, I have reason to think Bingley very much indebted to him."

"What is it you mean?"

"It is a circumstance which Darcy of course could not wish to be generally known, because if it were to get round to the lady's family; it would be an unpleasant thing."

"You may depend upon my not mentioning it."

"And remember that I have not much reason for supposing it to be Bingley. What he told me was merely this, that he congratulated himself on having lately saved a friend from a most imprudent marriage."

"Did Mr Darcy give you his reasons for this interference?"

"I understand that there were some very strong objections against the lady."

Later, shut into her own room, she could think without interruption of all that she had heard. So Mr Darcy's pride and conceit were the cause of all that Jane had suffered, and still continued to suffer. "There were some very strong objections against the lady," were Colonel Fitzwilliam's words, and those strong objections probably were, having one uncle who was a country attorney and another who was in business in London.

"To Jane herself," she exclaimed, "there could be no possibility of objection. All loveliness and goodness as she is!" The excitement and tears brought on a headache; it grew so much worse towards the evening that she was determined not to accompany her cousins to Rosings, where they were invited to drink tea.

11

A STRANGE PROPOSAL

When they were gone, Elizabeth re-read all the letters which Jane had written to her since her coming to Kent. In almost every line of each Jane's usual cheerfulness was missing. Mr Darcy's shameful boast of what misery he had been able to inflict gave her a keener sense of her sister's suffering.

She was suddenly roused by the sound of a doorbell and to her utter amazement she saw Mr Darcy walk into the room. In a hurried manner he immediately began an inquiry after her health, giving as the reason of his visit a wish to hear that she was better. She answered him coldly. He sat down for a few moments and then, getting up, walked about the room. Elizabeth was surprised but she didn't say a word. After a silence of a few minutes he came towards her in an agitated manner and began:

"In vain have I struggled. It will not do. My feeling will not be repressed. You must allow me to tell you how ardently I admire and love you."

Elizabeth's astonishment was beyond expression. She stared, coloured, doubted and was silent. He considered this sufficient encouragement, and the confession of all that he

---

proposal: offer of marriage
ardently: warmly, with strong feeling
confession: declaration

felt and had long felt for her immediately followed. He spoke well but he spoke of feelings other than of love and his pride overshadowed his feelings of tenderness towards her. His sense of her inferiority—of its being a degradation—of the family obstacles which judgement had always opposed, were dwelt on with a warmth which was very unlikely to recommend him.

She could not be insensible to the compliment of such a man's affection. But she lost all compassion in the anger which his subsequent language roused in her.

She tried to compose herself to answer him with patience. But he concluded by stating again the strength of that attachment which, in spite of all his efforts, he had found impossible to conquer. He expressed the hope that he would now be rewarded by her acceptance of his hand. As he said this, she could easily see that he had no doubt of a favourable answer. This angered her further, and, when he stopped, the colour rose into her cheeks, and she said,

"In such cases as this, I believe, it is customary to express gratitude for the sentiments shown even if they are not returned. It is natural that obligation should be felt, and if I could *feel* gratitude, I would now thank you. But I cannot—I have never desired your good opinion, and you have certainly given it most unwillingly. I am sorry to have caused pain to anyone. The feelings which you tell me, have long prevented the acknowledgement of your regard, can have little difficulty in overcoming it."

Mr Darcy, with eyes fixed on her face, seemed to catch her words with no less resentment than surprise. He became pale. He was struggling to appear calm. At length, in a voice of forced calmness, he said,

---

recommend him: make his proposal acceptable

acceptance of his hand: acceptance of his proposal of marriage

"And this is all the reply which I am to have the honour of expecting! I might, perhaps, wish to be informed why, I am rejected."

"I might as well inquire," replied she, "why with so evident a design of offending and insulting me, you chose to tell me that you liked me against your will, against your reason and even against your character. Was not this some excuse for incivility if I *was* incivil? But I have other causes. Do you think that any consideration would tempt me to accept the man who has been the means of ruining, perhaps for ever, the happiness of a most beloved sister?"

Mr Darcy changed colour, but he listened while she continued.

"I have every reason in the world to think ill of you. You cannot deny that you have been the principal, if not the only means, of dividing them from each other. Can you deny that you have done it?" she repeated.

Trying to be calm, he replied, "I have no wish of denying that I did everything in my power to separate my friend from your sister. Towards *him* I have been kinder than towards myself."

"But it is not merely this affair," she continued, "on which my dislike is founded. I came to know of your character in the account which I got many months ago from Mr Wickham. In what imaginary act of friendship can you here defend yourself?"

"You take an eager interest in that gentleman's affairs," said Mr Darcy less calmly, and with a heightened colour.

"Who that knows what his misfortunes have been, can help feeling an interest in him? You have reduced him to this present state of poverty. You have withheld the advantages which you must know to have been meant for him."

"And this," cried Darcy, as he walked with quick steps across the room, "is your opinion of me! My faults according to your calculation are heavy indeed! But perhaps," added he, stopping in his walk, and turning towards her, "these offences might have been overlooked, had not your pride been hurt by my honest confession of the reasons that had long prevented my speaking to you. Nor am I ashamed of my feelings. Could you expect me to rejoice in the inferiority of your connections?"

Elizabeth felt herself growing more angry every moment; yet she tried to speak with composure when she added,

"You could not have made me the offer of your hand in any possible way that could have tempted me to accept it."

His astonishment was obvious; and he looked at her with an expression mixed with disbelief and mortification. She went on.

"From the very first moment that I met you I became aware of your arrogance, your conceit, and your selfish indifference to the feelings of others. On this groundwork, succeeding events have built so immoveable a dislike, that I had not known you a month before I felt that you were the last man in the world whom I could marry."

"You have said quite enough, madam. I perfectly understand your feelings, and have now only to be ashamed of what my own have been. Forgive me for having taken up so much of your time, and accept my best wishes for your health and happiness."

And with these words he hastily left the room. The tumult of her mind was now painfully great, and from actual weakness she sat down and cried for half an hour. Her astonishment, as she reflected on what had passed, increased with every review of it. That she should receive an offer of marriage from Mr Darcy! That he was so much in love as to wish to marry her, in

---

connections: relations
the offer of your hand: your offer of marriage
mortification: humiliation
arrogance: overbearing manner or nature
tumult: great disturbance, confused state

spite of all objections which had made him prevent his friend's marrying her sister! All this was almost incredible. It was flattering to have roused so strong an affection. But his pride, his shameless admission of what he had done with respect to Jane, his cruelty towards Wickham, soon overcame the pity which the thought of his love and aroused for a moment.

She continued in very troubled reflections till the sound of Lady Catherine's carriage made her hurry away to her room, in order to avoid Charlotte.

12

Darcy's letter

Elizabeth awoke next morning to the same thoughts. She could not yet recover from the surprise of what had happened. She resolved soon after breakfast to take some exercise. After walking in the lane, she caught a glimpse of a gentleman, and fearing it was Mr Darcy, she turned away. But on hearing herself called, she moved again towards the gate. Holding out a letter, he said, "I have been walking in the grove some time in the hope of meeting you. Will you do me the honour of reading that letter?" And then, with a slight bow, turned and was soon out of sight.

Elizabeth opened the letter. It was dated from Rosings, at eight o'clock in the morning.

> *"Be not alarmed, madam. I write without any intention of paining you, or humbling myself by dwelling on wishes which, for the happiness of both, cannot be too soon forgotten. But my character required it to be written and read. You must, therefore, pardon the freedom with which I demand your attention. I demand it of your justice.*
>
> *Two offences of a very different nature, you last night laid to my charge. The first was, that, regardless of the feelings of either, I had separated Mr Bingley from your sister—and the*

---

grove: small wood, group of trees
do me the honour: a formal and polite way of saying please

other, that I had, in defiance of honour and humanity, ruined the immediate prosperity and prospects of Mr Wickham. But from the severity of the blame which was last night bestowed on me, I shall hope to be in future spared, when the following account of my actions and their motives has been read. If in the explanation of them, I have to describe feelings which may be offensive to yours, I can only say that I am sorry.

I had not been long in Hertfordshire, before I saw that Bingley preferred your elder sister to any other woman in the country. I had often seen him in love before. But it was at the dance at Netherfield that I first heard from Sir William Lucas that Bingley's attention to your sister had given rise to a general expectation of their marriage. From that moment I observed my friend's behaviour attentively; his preference for Miss Bennet was beyond what I had ever observed in him. Your sister I also watched. Her look and manners were open, cheerful and pleasing, but without any sign of special regard. Though she received his attentions with pleasure, she did not invite them by showing that she had the same feelings for him. If you have not been mistaken here I must have been in error. The serenity of your sister's behaviour was such as might have given the most careful observer a conviction that her heart was not likely to be easily touched.

My objections to the marriage were not merely those which I named last night. But there were other causes which I had myself tried to forget. The situation of your mother's family, though objectionable, was nothing in comparison of that total want of propriety so frequently shown by your mother and

---

serenity: calmness
propriety: proper and correct behaviour

three younger sisters and occasionally even by your father—pardon me. It pains me to offend you. But let it give you consolation to consider that you and your elder sister have always conducted yourselves so as to avoid any share of the same criticism.

Bingley left Netherfield for London on the following day, planning to return very soon. But his sisters' uneasiness was also roused, so we joined him in London, and there I pointed out to him the evils of such a choice. I do not suppose this wculd have prevented the marriage had I not assured him of your sister's indifference. Bingley has great natural modesty, with a stronger dependence on my judgement than on his own... To convince him, therefore, was no difficult matter.

There is one part of my conduct on which I do not reflect with satisfaction. It is that I concealed from him your sister's being in town. But if I have wounded your sister's feelings, it was unknowingly done.

With respect to the other accusation of having injured Mr Wickham, I can only refute it by laying before you the whole of his connection with my family. Mr Wickham is the son of a very respectable man, who had for many years the management of all my father's estates; and whose good conduct naturally made my father favour him, and his son George Wickham, who was my father's godson.

My father gave him a good education, and he had also a very high opinion of him. Hoping the church would be his profession, my father intended to provide for him in it. As for myself, I began to think of him in a very different manner,

---

refute it: prove it wrong

because of the want of principle, which could not escape the observation of a young man of nearly the same age, though my father could not know about it.

My excellent father died about five years ago. In his will he particularly recommended it to me, that if Wickham took orders, a valuable family living might be given to him as soon as it became vacant. There was also a legacy of one thousand pounds.

Within half a year, Mr Wickham wrote to inform me that he had resolved against taking orders. He had some intention of studying the law, but the interest of one thousand pounds would not be sufficient to support him. I knew that Mr Wickham ought not to be a clergyman. The business was therefore soon settled. He gave up all claim to assistance in the church, and accepted in return three thousand pounds. But his studying the law was a mere pretence. His life was a life of idleness and pleasure.

For about three years I heard little of him. He then wrote that his circumstances were exceedingly bad. He had found the law a most unprofitable study, and was now absolutely resolved on being ordained, if I would present him to the living which had just become vacant. You would hardly blame me for refusing to agree—and he was doubtless as violent in his abuse of me to others, as in his reproaches to myself. Then last summer he was again most painfully brought to my notice.

I must now mention a circumstance which I would wish to forget myself. I feel no doubt of your secrecy. My sister, who is more than ten years my junior, was left to the guardianship of

---

took orders: joined the church
circumstances: here, a person's financial position

my mother's nephew, Colonel Fitzwilliam, and myself. About a year ago, she was taken from school and a home set up for her in London in the care of Mrs Young. Last summer she went with this lady to Ramsgate, and there also went Mr Wickham, undoubtedly with a special purpose. As it was later revealed, he and Mrs Young were known to each other. We had been greatly deceived by her. He had recommended himself to Georgiana with her help. There he approached Georgiana, whose affectionate heart retained a strong impression of his kindness to her as a child. She was persuaded to believe herself in love, and to consent to run away from home and marry him. She was then but fifteen, which must be her excuse—I joined them unexpectedly a day or two before and then Georgiana, unable to bear the idea of grieving and offending a brother, whom she almost looked up to as a father, confessed the whole to me. You may imagine what I felt and how I acted. Regard for my sister prevented me from publicly exposing Mr Wickham. But I wrote to him and he left the place immediately and Mrs Young was relieved of her duties. Mr Wickham's chief object was unquestionably my sister's fortune, which is thirty thousand pounds; but I cannot help feeling that he also wanted to revenge himself on me. The revenge would have been complete indeed.

For the truth of everything here related, I can appeal to the testimony of Colonel Fitzwilliam, who was one of the executors of my father's will."

I will only add, "God bless you."

Fitzwilliam Darcy

Ramsgate: a popular holiday retreat on the southern coast of England
testimony: statement about the truth of something

Elizabeth eagerly went through the letter. She had begun with a strong prejudice against everything he might say. His objections to the match made her too angry to have any wish of doing him justice. He expressed no regret for what he had done. His style was haughty and insolent.

On the subject of Mr Wickham, she felt astonishment, fear, suspicion. She wanted to disbelieve it entirely, repeatedly exclaiming: "This must be false!" She compelled herself to read it again carefully. What Wickham had said of the living was fresh in her memory. It was impossible not to feel that there was deceit on one side or the other. But when she reread the particulars about his receiving in exchange so considerable a sum as three thousand pounds, she was forced to hesitate.

Every line proved clearly that it was possible Mr Darcy was entirely blameless throughout. Of Mr Wickham's former way of life, nothing had been known in Hertfordshire but what he told himself. She could see him before her, with his charming manners which had made him so popular everywhere. Alas! the story of his behaviour towards Miss Darcy received confirmation from what had passed between Colonel Fitzwilliam and herself only the morning before.

She remembered everything that had passed in conversation between Wickham and herself, in their first evening at Mr Philips's. She was now struck with the frankness of such communications to a stranger. She remembered that he had boasted of having no fear of seeing Mr Darcy, yet he had avoided the Netherfield ball the very next week. She remembered also that he had told his story to no one but herself. But after the Netherfield family went to town, it had been discussed everywhere. He had no misgivings about injuring Mr Darcy's character, though he had assured her that respect for the father would always prevent him exposing his son.

How differently everything appeared now. His attentions to Miss King showed his eagerness to grasp at anything. His behaviour towards herself might have been because he was misled about her fortune. On the other hand, proud and disagreeable as were Mr Darcy's manners, she had never seen anything that betrayed him to be unprincipled or unjust.

When she came to that part of the letter where her family was mentioned in terms of reproach, her sense of shame was severe because she knew the reproach was deserved. Of neither Darcy nor Wickham could she think, without feeling that she had been blind, partial, prejudiced, absurd.

Neither could she deny the justice of his description of Jane. She felt that it was true that Jane's feelings, though deep, were little displayed. She appreciated the compliment to herself and to her sister. When she considered that Jane's disappointment had in fact been the work of her nearest relations, Elizabeth felt deeply depressed.

The two gentlemen left Rosings the next morning. Consequently, Lady Catherine felt so dull that she asked the Collins family to dine with her. Elizabeth could not see Lady Catherine without recollecting that, had she chosen it, she might by this time have been presented to her as her future niece.

By now she nearly knew Mr Darcy's letter by heart. When she remembered the style of his proposal, she was still angry. But when she considered how unjustly she had condemned him, her anger was turned against herself. Her own behaviour distressed her. The unhappy defects of her family were the subject of yet heavier humiliation. Her family was beyond improvement. Her father, contented with laughing at them, would never exert himself to restrain the wild giddiness of his youngest daughters; and her mother was entirely unaware of the evil.

---

partial: showing too much favour to one side

giddiness: fondness of pleasure, without steady principles

Elizabeth and Jane had frequently tried to check the imprudence of Catherine and Lydia; but while they were supported by their mother's indulgence, what chance could there be of improvement? Lydia, self-willed and careless, would scarcely give them a hearing and Catherine was completely under Lydia's guidance. They were ignorant, idle and vain.

Anxiety on Jane's behalf was another cause of suffering. Mr Darcy's explanation had restored Bingley to her former good opinion; and this heightened the sense of what Jane had lost. A situation so desirable in every respect had been lost to Jane by the folly of her own family. Elizabeth's happy spirits, which had seldom been depressed before, were now so much affected as to make it almost impossible for her to appear cheerful.

---

indulgence: lack of control of another person's desires
folly: foolishness

13

LYDIA'S CAPERS CAUSE WORRY

On Saturday morning, Elizabeth left with Maria,

"Good gracious!" cried Maria, how much I will have to tell at home.

"And how much I will have to conceal," thought Elizabeth.

After staying at Mrs Gardiner's house for a few days, they returned with Jane to Hertfordshire. As they drew near the inn where Mr Bennet's carriage was to meet them, they saw Kitty and Lydia looking out of a dining room upstairs. Those two girls had been above an hour in the place, happily visiting a milliner opposite.

After welcoming their sisters, they triumphantly displayed a table set out with food, exclaiming: "Isn't this nice?"

"And we mean to treat you all," added Lydia, "but you must lend us the money, for we have just spent ours at the shop out there. Look, I have bought this bonnet."

And when her sisters said it was ugly, she agreed, but added, "It does not matter what one wears this summer, as the regiment is leaving in a fortnight."

"Are they indeed!" cried Elizabeth with the greatest satisfaction.

"They are going to be encamped near Brighton; and I do so want papa to take us there for the summer. Mamma would like to go too."

---

caper: frivolousness

"Yes," thought Elizabeth, "that would be a delightful scheme, indeed."

"Now I have some news for you," said Lydia. "There is no danger of Wickham's marrying Mary King. She has gone down to her uncle at Liverpool; Wickham is safe."

"And Mary King is safe!" added Elizabeth; "safe from a connection imprudent as to fortune."

As soon as all had eaten, the carriage was ordered. Their reception at home was most kind. Mrs Bennet rejoiced to see Jane looking so beautiful, and more than once during dinner did Mr Bennet say to Elizabeth.

"I am glad you are back, Lizzy."

Elizabeth could no longer contain her impatience to tell Jane what had happened. At length, resolving to suppress every particular in which her sister was concerned, and preparing her to be surprised, she related to her the next morning the chief details of the scene between Mr Darcy and herself.

Jane was sorry that Mr Darcy should have declared his love in a manner so little suited to recommend it; but still more was she grieved for the unhappiness which her sister's refusal must have given him. Elizabeth then spoke of the letter, repeating the whole of its contents as far as they concerned George Wickham. What a blow this was for poor Jane, who would willingly have gone through the world without believing in anybody's wickedness! How she wished that Darcy's character could have been cleared without hurting that of Wickham.

"There certainly was some great mismanagement in the education of those two young men. One has got all the goodness, and the other all the appearance of it," Elizabeth continued. "There is one point, on which I want your advice. I want to be told whether I ought, or ought not to make our acquaintances in general understand Wickham's character."

Jane paused a little and then replied, "Surely there can be no occasion for exposing him so dreadfully. What is your own opinion?"

"Mr Darcy has not authorised me to tell people. Moreover Wickham will soon be gone, and it will not matter to any of us here what he is," said Elizabeth. "At present I will not say anything about it."

"To have his errors made public might ruin him for ever. He is now, perhaps, sorry for what he has done and anxious to reform. We must not make him desperate."

Elizabeth's mind was set at ease after this conversation. But there was still something lingering behind. She dared not mention to her sister how sincerely she had been valued by Mr Bingley. Being now settled at home, she could observe the real state of her sister's spirits. Jane was not happy. She still cherished a tender affection for Bingley. Only her steady sense and sweetness of temper prevented her from indulging in her sorrow.

The week after their return was the last of the regiment's stay in Meryton, and all the young ladies in the neighbourhood were in low spirits. The elder Miss Bennets alone were still able to eat, drink, sleep and behave normally. Very frequently, they were reproached for their lack of feeling by Lydia and Kitty, whose own misery was extreme.

"If only one could go to Brighton!" observed Mrs Bennet.

"Oh, yes! But papa is so disagreeable."

But Lydia's gloom shortly cleared, for she received an invitation from Mrs Forster, the wife of the colonel of the regiment, to accompany her to Brighton. Mrs Forster was a very young woman, and very lately married.

Lydia's great joy on this occasion, the delight of Mrs Bennet, and the bitter disappointment of Kitty, are scarcely to be described.

Elizabeth could not help secretly advising her father not to let Lydia go. She represented to him how improper and unrefined Lydia's behaviour was. She would be yet more imprudent at Brighton, where the temptation must be greater than at home.

Mr Bennet saw that her whole heart was in the subject, and affectionately taking her hand, said in reply,

"Do not make yourself uneasy, my love. Wherever you and Jane are known, you must be respected and valued; and you will not appear to less advantage for having very silly sisters. We shall have no peace in Longbourn if Lydia does not go to Brighton. Let her go then. Colonel Forster is a sensible man, and will keep her out of any real mischief; and she is luckily too poor to be an object of prey to anybody."

With this answer Elizabeth was forced to be content, and she left him, disappointed and sorry.

On the regiment's very last day, Wickham dined at Longbourn. On his making some inquiry about Hunsford, Elizabeth mentioned that Colonel Fitzwilliam and Mr Darcy had both spent three weeks at Rosings, and asked him if he knew the former.

Wickham looked surprised, displeased, alarmed; then with a moment's recollection and a returning smile replied that he had formerly seen him often; and that he was a gentleman. He asked how she had liked him. She answered warmly in his favour.

Wickham's alarm seemed increased. They parted at last with mutual greetings and possibly a mutual desire of never meeting again.

14

Elizabeth starts out on a holiday

Elizabeth's father had married her mother, charmed by her youth and beauty, and that appearance of good humour which youth and beauty generally give. But Mrs Bennet's lack of intelligence and good sense and her small-mindedness had very early in their marriage put an end to all real affection for her. Respect, esteem and confidence had vanished for ever. But Mr Bennet was fond of the country and of books; and from these tastes had arisen his principal enjoyments. His wife's ignorance and folly only provided him with amusement.

Elizabeth, however, had never been blind to the impropriety of her father's behaviour as a husband. She had always seen it with pain but respecting his cleverness and intelligence and grateful for his affection for her, she tried to forget what she could not overlook. She had never felt so strongly as now the disadvantages which the children of so unsuitable a marriage suffer.

Elizabeth's tour to the Lakes was now the object of her happiest thoughts. A fortnight before the tour was to begin a letter arrived from Mrs Gardiner. Mr Gardiner would be prevented by business from setting out till much later, and

---

impropriety: lack of correctness, unsuitable behaviour

must be in London again within a month. So they would have to give up the Lakes, but intended to have a shorter holiday in Derbyshire. Elizabeth was extremely disappointed. It was impossible for her to see Derbyshire without thinking of Pemberley and its owner.

At last they set off on their holiday, while the four small Gardiner children were left at Longbourn in Jane's care. Presently they came to the little town of Lambton, where Mrs Gardiner had lived before her marriage, and still had some old friends. While at Lambton her aunt expressed a desire to see Pemberley. Elizabeth was distressed, because of the possibility of meeting Mr Darcy, while viewing the place. She thought it would be better to speak openly to her aunt than to run such a risk. But before doing so, she would privately inquire whether the family was staying at Pemberley.

Accordingly, when she went to bed at night, she asked the chambermaid whether the family was down for the summer. A most welcome negative followed the question, so she agreed to visit Pemberley next day.

As they drove along, Elizabeth watched for the first appearance of Pemberley woods, with some anxiety.

The park was very large and offered a great variety. They entered it and drove through a beautiful wood. Elizabeth's mind was too full for conversation, but she saw and admired every remarkable spot and point of view. Pemberley House was situated on the opposite side of a valley. It was a large, handsome stone building, standing well on rising ground, and backed by a ridge of high woody hills; and, in front a flowing stream. Elizabeth was delighted.

They were shown round the great house by the housekeeper, Mrs Reynolds, an elderly woman with pleasant manners. The rooms were lofty and handsome, and the furniture suitable to the fortune of their owner. In many of the rooms Elizabeth stopped at the window to look out on beautiful views.

"And of this place," thought Elizabeth, "I might have been mistress! Instead of visiting it as a stranger, I might have been familiarly acquainted with it, and might have welcomed my uncle and aunt as visitors to it. But no—that could never be: my uncle and aunt would have been lost to me. I should not have been allowed to invite them." This was a lucky recollection—it saved her from something like regret.

Her aunt now called her to look at a picture. Mrs Reynolds told them it was the picture of a young gentleman, the son of her late master's steward, who had been brought up by him. "He is now gone into the army," she added "but I am afraid he has turned out very wild."

"And that," said Mrs Reynolds, pointing to another, "is my master. And don't you think him a very handsome gentleman, ma'am?"

"Yes, very handsome."

"Is your master much at Pemberley in the course of the year?" asked Mr Gardiner.

"Not as much as I could wish, sir; but he is coming tomorrow with a party."

"If your master would marry, you might see more of him."

"Yes, sir; but I do not know when that will be. I do not know who is good enough for him."

Elizabeth could not help saying, "It is very much to his credit, I am sure, that you should think so."

"I say no more than the truth, and what everybody will say that knows him," replied Mrs Reynolds. Elizabeth listened with increasing astonishment as the house keeper added, "I have never had a cross word from him in my life, and I have known him since he was four years old."

This was praise, of all others most extraordinary, most opposite to her ideas. Her keenest attention was awakened, she longed to hear more, and was grateful to her uncle for saying.

"You are lucky in having such a master."

"Yes, sir, I know I am. In his childhood he was always the sweetest-tempered, most generous-hearted boy in the world."

Elizabeth almost stared at her, "Can this be Mr Darcy!" she thought. She listened, wondered, doubted, and was impatient for more.

"He is the best landlord and the best master," said Mrs Reynolds, "as all his tenants and his servants will assure you." She then showed them a very pretty sitting room, lately fitted up with great elegance for Miss Darcy. "And this is always the way with him," she added, "whatever can give his sister any pleasure is sure to be done in a moment. There is nothing he would not do for her."

This aroused in Elizabeth's mind a more gentle feeling for Mr Darcy than she had ever felt before. As a brother, a landlord, a master, she considered how many people's happiness was in his guardianship! How much pleasure or pain it was in his power to bestow! She thought of his regard with a deeper feeling of gratitude than ever before. She remembered its warmth, and softened its impropriety of expression.

As they were walking again towards the river and as her uncle was guessing the date of the building, the owner himself suddenly came forward from the road. They were within twenty yards of each other, and so sudden was his appearance that it was impossible to avoid him. Their eyes met and both blushed deeply. He absolutely started, but recovering himself spoke to Elizabeth.

Elizabeth was more embarrassed and confused than she had ever been before. The impropriety of her being found there made those few moments the most uncomfortable of her life. He seemed equally embarrassed, but he made inquiries after herself, and to her great surprise after her family. At length he suddenly recollected himself, and look leave.

Elizabeth was overpowered by shame and vexation. Oh! why had she come to Pemberley, or why did he thus come unexpected, for it was plain from the gardener's surprise that he had at that moment arrived. She blushed again and again over the awkwardness of the meeting. And his behaviour was so strikingly altered! That he should speak to her was amazing! Never had he spoken with such gentleness as at this unexpected meeting.

They entered the woods. The others now joined her and they went along the accustomed route which brought them again to the edge of the river. Her aunt was no great walker, and as they were wandering slowly they were again surprised by the sight of Mr Darcy approaching them. Elizabeth was astonished but resolved to appear composed and speak calmly, so she made a few remarks about the beauty of the place.

Mr Darcy then asked if she would do him the honour of introducing him to her friends. This was something for which she was quite unprepared; she could hardly suppress a smile. "What will be his surprise," thought she, "when he knows who they are! He takes them now for people of fashion."

That he was *surprised* by the relationship was evident. So far from going away he turned back with them and entered into conversation with Mr Gardiner. She heard Mr Darcy invite her uncle to fish there as often as he chose. Elizabeth's astonishment was extreme; "Why is he so altered?" she repeated. "It is impossible that he should still love me."

She wished him to know that she had been assured of his absence before she came to the place, so she remarked that his arrival must have been unexpected, as the housekeeper had said he was not coming till the next day. He replied that business with his steward had made him come a few hours earlier. The rest of the party was coming the next day and among them were Mr Bingley and his sisters.

"There is also one other person in the party," he continued, "who more particularly wishes to be known to you. Will you allow me to introduce my sister to you during your stay in Lambton?"

The surprise of such a request was great indeed; it was too great for her to know in what manner she agreed to it. He pressed them all to go into the house and take some refreshments. They declined and parted politely.

On the way back Mrs Gardiner spoke about Mr Darcy. "From what we have seen of him, I really should not have thought that he could have behaved in so cruel a way as he has done to poor Wickham."

Elizabeth now felt that she had to say something in defence of Mr Darcy's behaviour to Wickham. She therefore gave them to understand, in as guarded a manner as she could, that Mr Darcy's character was by no means so faulty or Wickham's so amiable as they had believed.

The next morning, Miss Darcy and her brother appeared at the inn where Elizabeth was staying, and the introductions were made. She had heard that Miss Darcy was exceedingly proud; in a few minutes she was convinced that she was only exceedingly shy. Miss Darcy was tall, and though she was only sixteen her appearance was womanly and graceful. Her manners were perfectly unassuming and gentle.

Mr Bingley followed a few minutes later. He greeted her with unaffected cordiality. Mr and Mrs Gardiner had of course long wished to see him. But the whole party roused their interest. As they observed Mr Darcy and their niece, Mr Darcy showed himself most anxious to please, and free from reserve and a sense of his own importance. Their observations convinced them that one of the two at least knew what it was to love. Of the lady's feelings they remained a little in doubt.

On seeing Bingley, Elizabeth's thoughts flew to her sister. She watched his behaviour to Miss Darcy, who had been set up

---

unaffected cordiality: sincere friendliness

as a rival to Jane. Nothing occurred between them that could justify the hopes of his sister. At a moment when the others were talking together, he said in a tone of real regret, that it was a very long time since he had the pleasure of seeing her sister. Before she could reply, he added, "It is above eight months. We have not met since the 26th of November, when we were all dancing together at Netherfield." This pleased Elizabeth very much.

Before their visitors rose to depart, they invited Mr and Mrs Gardiner and Elizabeth to dinner at Pemberley; and the day after the next was fixed on. Mr Gardiner was also specially invited to go fishing with the gentlemen at Pemberley.

In the evening it was settled between aunt and niece that the courtesy shown by Miss Darcy in coming to them ought to be repaid, and consequently they would call on her at Pemberley next morning.

Mrs Gardiner had heard from her friends at Lambton that, when Wickham quitted Derbyshire, he had left many debts behind him which Mr Darcy had paid; and this again confirmed her good opinion of Mr Darcy.

On reaching Pemberley House, they were received by Miss Darcy, who was sitting there with Mrs Hurst, Miss Bingley and Mrs Annesley, the lady with whom she lived in London. Georgiana's reception of them was very polite, but she was very shy; and this could have led to the belief that she was proud and reserved. Mrs Gardiner and her niece, however, did her justice, and pitied her.

Elizabeth soon saw that she was herself closely watched by Miss Bingley, who however would not take any part in the conversation. After a quarter of an hour she asked briefly after the health of Elizabeth's family. Elizabeth's answer was just as brief. Soon a servant entered with refreshments. The beautiful peaches and bunches of grapes soon collected them around the table.

While they were eating, Mr Darcy, who had been fishing with Mr Gardiner, entered. Elizabeth saw that the suspicions of the whole party were awakened towards them. It was Miss Bingley who watched with the most attentive and jealous curiosity, for she still hoped to win Mr Darcy's affection. At last she imprudently showed her anger by saying with sneering civility,

"Pray, Miss Eliza, are not the soldiers removed from Meryton? They must be a great loss to *your* family."

In Darcy's presence she dared not mention Wickham's name; but Elizabeth knew that he was uppermost in her thoughts. With an effort she answered the ill-natured attack calmly. An involuntary glance showed her that Darcy was earnestly looking at her, while his sister was overcome with confusion. Miss Bingley evidently did not know what pain she was giving her beloved friend. She had merely intended to embarrass Elizabeth, and perhaps to remind Darcy of all the follies of her family.

Their visit did not continue long afterwards, and while Mr Darcy was attending them to their carriage, Miss Bingley was criticising Elizabeth's behaviour and dress. But Georgiana could not join her. Her brother had spoken in such terms of Elizabeth that Georgiana could not but find her other than lovely and amiable.

15

The Elopement

Elizabeth was eagerly expecting a letter from Jane. On the third morning she received two letters from her at once, one of which, written five days ago, had been misdirected. She opened this first. The beginning contained news of parties and the like, but the latter half, which was dated a day later, and written in evident agitation, gave more important news, Jane wrote,

An express came at twelve last night, just as we had all gone to bed, from Colonel Forster, to inform us that Lydia had gone off to Scotland with Wickham! Imagine our surprise. I am very, very sorry. So imprudent a match on both sides! His choice is disinterested at least, for he must know that my father can give her nothing. Our poor mother is sadly grieved. My father bears it better.

On finishing this letter Elizabeth instantly opened the other. It had been written a day later and read:

Imprudent as a marriage between Mr Wickham and our poor Lydia would be, we are now anxious to be assured it has taken place; for there is but too much reason to fear otherwise. On hearing Denny say that he did not think Wickham intended to marry Lydia at all, Colonel Forster was greatly alarmed and set off to trace their route. He did trace them to Clapham but no further. Our distress, my dear Lizzy, is very great. My father and mother believe the worst, but I cannot think so ill of him. I never in my life saw my father so disturbed. I cannot help earnestly begging you all to come here as soon as possible. My father is going to London with Colonel Forster instantly to try to discover Lydia. In such circumstances my uncle's advice and assistance would be everything in the world; I am confident that we can rely upon his goodness to assist my father.

"Oh! Where is my uncle?" cried Elizabeth jumping from her chair. But as she reached the door, it was opened by a servant and Mr Darcy appeared. Her pale face and impetuous manner made him start.

"I beg your pardon," she said, "I must find Mr Gardiner, I have not an instant to lose."

"Good God! What is the matter?" cried he with more feeling than politeness. Then, recollecting himself, "I will not detain you a minute, but let me or let the servant go after Mr and Mrs Gardiner. You are not well enough; you cannot go yourself."

Elizabeth's knees trembled under her; she sent the servant in search of her uncle and aunt, and sat down. She was looking so miserably ill, that it was impossible for Darcy to leave her. In a tone of gentleness he said, "Let me call your maid—you are very ill."

"No, I thank you," she replied, trying to recover herself. "I am quite well, I am only distressed by some dreadful news which I have just received from Longbourn."

She burst into tears as she added, "My youngest sister has eloped—has thrown herself in the power of Mr Wickham. They have gone off together from Brighton. She has no money, no connections, nothing that can tempt him to—she is lost

---

impetuous: quick and violent
eloped: run away with a lover

forever. When I consider," she added in a yet more agitated voice, "that *I* might have prevented it, I who knew what he was. Had I only explained some part of what I had learnt, to my own family, this could not have happened. But it is all too late now."

"I am grieved and shocked indeed," cried Darcy. "What has been done to recover her?"

"My father has gone to London and Jane has written asking my uncle's immediate help. We shall be off, I hope, in half an hour. But how is such a man to be worked on? I have not the smallest hope."

Darcy seemed scarcely to hear her and was walking up and down the room in gloomy meditation. Elizabeth soon observed this and instantly understood it. Her influence over him was decreasing, as was natural under such an assurance of the deepest disgrace. She could neither wonder at his behaviour nor condemn him for his thoughts about her family; and never had she so honestly felt that she could have loved him, as now, when all love must be in vain.

The humiliation which Lydia was bringing to them all soon swallowed up every private care; and covering her face with her handkerchief, Elizabeth was soon lost to everything else. She was recalled to a sense of her situation by the voice of her companion. He spoke with sympathy and likewise restraint, "Would to Heaven that anything could be either said or done on my part that might offer consolation to such distress. This unfortunate affair will, I fear, prevent my sister's having the pleasure of seeing you at Pemberley today."

"Oh, yes. Be so kind as to apologise for us to Miss Darcy. Conceal the unhappy truth as long as it is possible."

He readily assured her of his secrecy, expressed his sorrow at her distress, and his wish that it should have a happier conclusion than seemed possible just then. Then, with only one serious parting look, he went way.

As he left the room, Elizabeth felt with great regret how improbable it was that they should ever see each other again on such friendly terms as their meetings in Derbyshire. She turned now to her thoughts to Lydia. She did not suppose that Lydia would elope without the intention of marrying. But she had no difficulty in believing that neither her virtue nor her understanding would preserve her from falling an easy prey to the designs of a wicked man. Lydia was so thoughtless and anxious for amusement and adventure. How keenly she felt the mischief of neglect and mistaken indulgence to such a girl!

Mr and Mrs Gardiner hurried back in alarm, and Elizabeth eagerly read the two letters to them aloud. Mr Gardiner promised every assistance in his power. They were to be off as soon as possible.

"But what is to be done about Pemberley?" cried Mrs Gardiner.

"Yes, I told Mr Darcy we should not be able to keep our engagement. *That* is all settled."

"Are they upon such terms as for her to disclose the real truth?" wondered Mrs Gardiner.

They completed all their preparations within an hour, and were in the carriage and on the road to Longbourn.

They travelled as quickly as possible, and reached Longbourn by dinner time the next day. Elizabeth jumped out, affectionately embraced Jane, and asked whether anything had been heard of Lydia and Wickham.

"Not yet," replied Jane. "But now that my dear uncle has come, I hope everything will be well. My father has gone to London. He will not write again until there is something of importance to mention."

Mrs Bennet, to whose room they all then went, received them exactly as might be expected; with tears and lamentations,

---

preserve her: keep her safe

violent abuse of Wickham and complaints concerning her own suffering and ill-treatment. As usual, she blamed everybody but herself.

Mr Gardiner told her that he meant to be in London the very next day, and would assist Mr Bennet in every effort for recovering Lydia.

"Oh! my dear brother," replied Mrs Bennet, "find them out, and if they are not married already, *make* them marry. And as for wedding clothes, tell Lydia she shall have as much money as she chooses to buy them, after they are married. Keep Mr Bennet from fighting. Tell him what a dreadful state I am in. I can get no rest by night or day. And tell Lydia not to give any directions about the clothes till she has seen me."

In the afternoon the two elder Miss Bennets were able to be by themselves for half an hour. Jane told Elizabeth all that had happened in the last few days.

"And did Colonel Forster appear to think ill of Wickham himself? Does he know his real character?" asked Elizabeth.

"He did not speak so well of Wickham as he formerly did. He believed him to be imprudent and extravagant, and it is said that he left Meryton greatly in debt."

"Oh, Jane, had we been less secretive, this could not have happened. Could Colonel Forster tell you what Lydia wrote to Mrs Forster when she left?"

"He brought her letter with him for us to see," said Jane and handed it to Elizabeth. These were the contents:

My dear Harriet,

You will laugh when you know I am gone, and I cannot help laughing myself at your surprise tomorrow morning. If you cannot guess with whom, I shall think you a simpleton, for there is one man in the world I love, and he is an angel. You need not send them word at Longbourn of my going, if you do not like it, for it will make the surprise the greater, when I write to them, and sign my name Lydia Wickham. What a good joke it will be! I shall send for my clothes when I get to Longbourn; but I wish you would tell Sally to mend a great slit in my muslin gown, before they are packed up. Goodbye. I hope you will drink to our good journey.

Your affectionate friend,
Lydia Bennet.

"Oh! thoughtless, thoughtless Lydia!" cried Elizabeth. "What a letter is this to be written at such a moment. But at least it shows that *she* was serious in the object of her journey. My poor father! How he must have felt it!"

Mrs Gardiner stayed in Hertfordshire a few days longer and was a great comfort to them all. After Mr Gardiner left Longbourn his wife received a letter before she joined him. He wrote that Mr Bennet had not yet found Lydia and Wickham and he was totally disinclined at present to leave London; they were trying to find whether Wickham had any relations who would be able to help! Every day at Longbourn was now a day of anxiety.

Mr Gardiner did not write again, till he had received an answer from Colonel Forster. It was not known that Wickham had a single relation. There was no one therefore who could be likely to give any news of him. Besides he had left gaming debts behind him of about a thousand pounds. Mr Gardiner added that they might expect to see their father at home on the following day. Rendered spiritless by the ill-success of all their endeavours, he had yielded to his brother-in-law's request, and would leave it to him to do whatever the occasion might suggest.

---

gaming: gambling

"What, is he coming home and without poor Lydia?" Mrs Bennet cried when she head about it. "Who is to fight Wickham and make him marry Lydia, if he comes away?"

When Mr Bennet arrived he had all the appearance of his usual philosophical composure. Elizabeth expressed sorrow for what he must have endured. "Say nothing of that," he replied. "It has been my own doing and I ought to feel it. Let me once in my life feel how much I am to blame."

16

An agreement

Two days after his return, Mr Bennet received a letter by express from Mr Gardiner.

"Is it good news or bad?" asked Elizabeth eagerly.

"What is there of good to be expected?" said her father. "Read it aloud, for I hardly know myself what it is about."

Gracechurch Street, Monday
August 2

My dear Brother,

At last I am able to send you some tidings of my niece, and such as, upon the whole, I hope will give you satisfaction. I have seen them both. They are not married, nor can I find there was any intention of being so; but if you are willing to agree to the promise which I have ventured to make on your side, I hope it will not be long before they are. All that is required of you is to assure to your daughter, by settlement, her equal share of the five thousand pounds secured among your children after the decease of yourself and my sister; and moreover, to enter into an engagement to allow her, during your life, one hundred pounds per annum. You will easily comprehend, from

---

tidings: news
decease: death
engagement: promise, especially one that is formal or in writing

these particulars, that Mr Wickham's circumstances are not so hopeless as they are generally believed to be; and I am happy to say there will be some little money, even when all his debts are discharged, to settle on my niece, in addition to her own fortune. If you send me full powers to act in your name, I will immediately give directions to the lawyer for preparing a proper settlement. We have judged it best that my niece should be married from this house. She comes to us today.

Yours, etc.
Ed. Gardiner

"Wickham is not so undeserving, then, as we have thought him," said Jane.

"And have you answered the letter?" said Elizabeth.

"It must be done," he replied. "But there are two things that I want very much to know: one is, how much money your uncle has laid down, to bring it about; and the other, how I am ever to pay him."

"Money! my uncle!" cried Jane. "What do you mean, sir?"

"Wickham's a fool if he takes her with a farthing less than ten thousand pounds. How is half such a sum to be repaid?"

Then he went to the library to write.

"And they are really to be married!" cried Elizabeth. "And for *this* we are to be thankful."

"I comfort myself with thinking," replied Jane, "that he certainly would not marry Lydia, if he had not a real regard for her. Though our kind uncle has done something towards clearing him, I cannot believe that ten thousand pounds, or anything like it, has been advanced."

"The kindness of my uncle and aunt can never be repaid. Their taking her home, and affording her their personal protection, is so much to her advantage. By this time she is actually with them!" said Elizabeth.

"We must try and forget all that passed on either side," said Jane. "I hope and trust that they will yet be happy. His consenting to marry her is a proof, I will believe, that he has come to a right way of thinking."

It now occurred to the girls that their mother was ignorant of what had happened.

They went upstairs together with the letter. Mrs Bennet could hardly restrain herself. Her joy burst forth. She was disturbed by no fear for Lydia's happiness, nor humbled by any remembrance of her misconduct.

"My dear, dear Lydia!" she cried. "This is delightful indeed! She will be married at sixteen. But the wedding clothes! I will write to my sister Gardiner about them immediately. Lizzy, my dear, run down to your father, and ask him how much he will give her." She then proceeded to all the particulars of calico, muslin and cambric.

"I will go to Meryton," said she, "and tell the good, good news to my sister Philips. And as I come back, I can call on Lady Lucas and Mrs Long."

Mr Bennet had very often wished, before this period of his life, that, instead of spending his whole income, he had laid by an annual sum for the better provision of his children, and his wife. Had he done his duty, Lydia need not have been indebted to her uncle for whatever of honour could now be purchased for her. In his letter he begged to know further particulars of how much he was indebted to his brother, but was too angry with Lydia to send any message to her.

Mrs Bennet took her seat once again at the head of her table and in high spirits. No sentiment of shame decreased her triumph. Her thoughts and her words were wholly about fine muslins, new carriages, and a proper house in the neighbourhood for Lydia to settle in.

"Mrs Bennet," said Mr Bennet, "before you take any or all of these houses, let us come to a right understanding. Into *one* house in this neighbourhood they shall never have admittance. I will not receive them at Longbourn."

A long dispute followed this declaration; but Mr Bennet was firm; and Mrs Bennet found with amazement and horror that her husband would not advance a guinea to buy clothes for his daughter. She was more alive to the disgrace which the want of new clothes must reflect on her daughter's marriage than any sense of shame at her eloping and living with Wickham a fortnight before the marriage.

Elizabeth was now most heartily sorry that she had from the distress of the moment made Mr Darcy acquainted with their fears for her sister, since her marriage shortly would conceal its unfavourable beginning.

She had no fears of its spreading further. There were few people on whose secrecy she would have more confidently depended. But at the same time, there was no one whose knowledge of a sister's weakness would have mortified her so much. Had Lydia married on the most honourable terms, Mr Darcy would have had nothing to do with a family, where to every other objection would now be added a near relationship with a man whom he so justly scorned. She was humbled and grieved. She began now to comprehend that he was exactly the man who in character and talents would most suit her.

Mr Gardiner soon wrote again. He expressed his eagerness to promote the welfare of any of his family and requested that the subject of repayment might never be mentioned again. He specially mentioned that Mr Wickham had resolved to join a regiment stationed in the north, and that before leaving Lydia was very anxious to see her parents and sisters.

Lydia's request at first received an absolute negative from Mr Bennet. But Jane and Elizabeth urged their father so earnestly, yet so reasonably and so mildly to receive her and her husband at Longbourn, that he was persuaded to act as they wished.

17

Lydia and Wickham at Longbourn

Their sister's wedding day arrived; and Jane and Elizabeth felt for her probably more than she felt for herself. The carriage was sent to meet Lydia and Wickham, and they were to come by dinner time. They came. Smiles decked the face of Mrs Bennet, her husband looked impenetrably grave; her daughters, alarmed, anxious, uneasy. Lydia's voice was heard outside; her mother stepped forward, embraced her, and welcomed her with rapture. She gave her hand with an affectionate smile to Wickham, who followed his lady.

Their reception by Mr Bennet was not so cordial; he scarcely opened his lips. The easy assurance of the young couple, indeed, was enough to provoke him. Elizabeth was disgusted, and even Jane was shocked. Lydia was Lydia still untamed, wild, noisy, and fearless.

The bride and her mother could neither of them talk fast enough.

"Only think of its being three months," Lydia cried, "since I went away. Good gracious! when I went away, I am sure I had no idea of being married, though I thought it would be very good fun if I was."

Her father lifted up his eyes, Jane was distressed, Elizabeth looked expressively at Lydia; but she gaily continued, "Oh!

---

impenetrably grave: so serious that his feelings could not be made out from his face

mamma, do the people hereabouts know I am married today? I was afraid they might not; so when we saw Mr Goulding I put my hand out in such a way that he might see the ring."

When they went in to dinner Lydia walked up to her mother's right hand and said, "Ah, Jane, I take your place now, and you must go lower, because I am a married woman."

"Well, mamma," said she, when they all returned to the breakfast room, "and what do you think of my husband? Isn't he a charming man? I am sure my sisters must all envy me. I only hope they may have half my good luck."

"I do not particularly like your way of getting husbands," said Elizabeth sharply.

Wickham behaved with his usual easy good manners which had made him seem so likable before they discovered his real character. Elizabeth noticed that his affection for Lydia was not equal to Lydia's for him. She felt that he would not have eloped with Lydia, had his flight not been necessary because of his debts.

One morning, soon after her arrival, Lydia said to Elizabeth,

"Lizzy, I never gave *you* an account of my wedding. We were to be married at St Clements. My uncle and aunt and I were to go together; and the others were to meet us at the church. Well, Monday morning came, and I was in such a fuss! And there was my aunt, all the time I was dressing, preaching and talking away just as if she were reading a sermon. However, I did not hear above one word in ten, for I longed to know whether Wickham would be married in his blue coat. Well, just as the carriage came to the door, my uncle was called away upon business. I did not know what to do, for my uncle was to give me away. However, I recollected afterwards, that if he *had* been prevented from coming in time, Mr Darcy might have done as well."

"My Darcy!" repeated Elizabeth in utter amazement.

"Oh, yes—he was to come there with Wickham, you know. But gracious me! I quite forgot. It was to be such a secret."

"If it was to be a secret," said Jane, "do not say another word on the subject."

But to live in ignorance on such a point was impossible for Elizabeth. Questions as to the meaning of it, rapid and wild, hurried into her brain; but she was satisfied with none. She could not bear such suspense; and hastily seizing a sheet of paper, wrote a short letter to her aunt, to request an explanation of what Lydia had dropped, if it was compatible with the secrecy which had been intended.

Elizabeth had the satisfaction of receiving a speedy answer to her letter. Mrs Gardiner wrote:

Gracechurch Street, Sept. 6

My dear niece,

I am surprised by your request, for I had not imagined such inquiries to be necessary from your side. Your uncle is as much surprised as I am—and nothing but the belief of your being a party concerned would have allowed him to act as he has done. But if you are really ignorant I must explain.

On the very day of my coming home from Longbourn, Mr Darcy called and was shut up with your uncle for several hours. He came to tell Mr Gardiner that he had found out where your sister and Mr Wickham were, and that he had talked with them both. The motive professed was that he felt it was his own fault that Wickham's worthlessness had not been so well known as to make it impossible for any young woman of character to love or trust him. He generously imputed the whole to his own mistaken pride. He confessed that he had before thought it beneath him to lay his private actions open to the world. He felt it, therefore, his duty to endeavour to remedy the evil which had been brought on by himself. If he had another motive, I am sure it would never disgrace him. He tried to persuade Lydia to quit her present disgraceful situation and return to her friends. But she would not hear of leaving her dear Wickham. She was sure they would be married some time or other and it did not much matter when. Darcy learnt in his very first conversation with Wickham that marriage with Lydia had never been his intention. Wickham still hoped to make his fortune by a rich marriage, in some other country.

However, he was not likely to be proof against the temptation of an immediate offer of money. They met several times. Wickham of course wanted more than what he could get, but at length was persuaded to be reasonable.

Our visitor was very obstinate. I fancy, Lizzy, that obstinacy is the real defect of his character after all. Nothing was to be done that he did not do himself. Your uncle would have readily settled the whole. But at last your uncle was forced to yield; and to put up with only having the credit of it. Your letter this morning gave him great pleasure because it required an explanation that would rob him of his borrowed feathers, and give the praise where it was due. But, Lizzy, this must go no further than yourself, or Jane at most. You know what has been done for the young people. His debts are to be paid, amounting, I believe, to more than a thousand pounds, another thousand in addition to her own settled upon her, and his commission purchased. Mr Darcy again repeated the reason why this should be paid by him alone. It was owing to him, to

---

commission purchased: for a long time officers in the British army had to pay money to buy the rank of an officer

his reserve, and want of proper consideration, that Wickham's character had been so misunderstood, and consequently, that he had been received and noticed as he was. But your uncle would never have yielded if we had not given Mr Darcy credit for another interest in the affair.

Mr Darcy then returned to Pemberley. But it was agreed that he would return when the wedding took place. He was punctual and as Lydia informed you attended the wedding. Will you be very angry with me, my dear Lizzy, if I take this opportunity of saying how much I like him? His understanding and his opinions all please me; he wants nothing but a little more liveliness, and that, if he marry prudently, his wife may teach him.

Yours very sincerely,
M. Gardiner

The contents of the letter threw Elizabeth into a flutter of spirits, in which it was difficult to determine whether pleasure or pain bore the greatest share. Darcy had followed them purposely to town, he had taken on himself all the trouble attendant on such a search; in which persuasion had been necessary with people whom he must despise. He was forced to meet frequently, reason with, persuade, and finally bribe, the man whom he always most wished to avoid. But he had given a reason for his interference, which it was not impossible to believe. She could perhaps believe that love for her might have been an additional reason.

It was exceedingly painful to know that they were under obligations to a person who could never receive a return. Oh! how heartily did she grieve about her unkind feelings towards him, and her sharp replies to him. For herself she was humbled; but she was proud of him. She read her aunt's praise of him again and again.

18

Jane is engaged

The day of Mr Wickham's and Lydia's departure soon came.

"Oh! my dear Lydia," cried Mrs Bennet, "when shall we meet again? Write to me very often, my dear."

"As often as I can. But you know married women have never much time for writing. My sisters may write to *me*. They will have nothing else to do."

Mr Wickham's farewells were much more affectionate than his wife's. He smiled, looked handsome, and said many pleasant things.

The loss of her daughter made Mrs Bennet very dull for several days. But the spiritless condition was shortly relieved by the news that the housekeeper at Netherfield had received orders to prepare for the arrival of her master.

Jane had not been able to hear of his coming, without changing colour. Elizabeth did not know what to make of his coming. She could easily perceive that Jane's spirits were affected by the news.

On the third morning after his arrival in Hertfordshire, Mrs Bennet saw Mr Bingley ride towards the house. Mr Darcy was with him. Jane looked at Elizabeth with surprise and concern. Both sisters were uncomfortable enough. But Elizabeth's cause of uneasiness could not be suspected by Jane. She had never yet had courage to show Jane Mrs Gardiner's letter, or relate her own change of feelings towards him. He was the person to whom the whole family was indebted and whom she regarded with a tender interest. She was astonished at his coming, and voluntarily seeking her again.

On the gentlemen's appearing, Jane's colour increased, yet she received them with ease. Elizabeth said as little to either as politeness would allow.

Darcy inquired of her how Mr and Mrs Gardiner were, a question which she could not answer without confusion. He said very little but when she raised her eyes to his face, she found him looking as often at Jane as at herself, and frequently at no object but the ground. More thoughtfulness and less anxiety to please than when they last met were plainly expressed. She was disappointed, and angry with herself for being so. She inquired after his sister but could do no more. Mrs Bennet was telling Mr Bingley about Lydia's happy marriage and how they were gone to Newcastle.

"I suppose you have heard about it; indeed you must have seen it in the papers. Thank Heaven! he has *some* friends, though, perhaps, not so many as he deserves," she said.

Elizabeth, who knew this to be levelled at Mr Darcy, was in such misery of shame, that she could hardly keep her seat. She observed how her sister's beauty aroused the admiration of her former lover. He found her as handsome as she had been last year; as good-natured, and as unaffected, though not quite so chatty.

When the gentlemen rose to go away, Mrs Bennet invited them to dine at Longbourn in a few days' time. She had been inclined to ask them to stay and dine that very day but did not think anything less than two courses could be good enough for a man on whom she had such anxious designs, or satisfy the pride and appetite of one who had ten thousand a year.

On Tuesday there was a large party assembled at Longbourn and the two who were most anxiously expected were in good time. When they repaired to the dining room,Elizabeth eagerly watched to see whether Bingley would take the place which, in all their former parties, had belonged to him, by her sister. Her prudent mother, occupied by the same ideas, forebore to invite him to sit by herself. On entering the room, he seemed to hesitate, but Jane happened to look round, and happened to smile; it was decided. He placed himself by her.

Elizabeth, with a triumphant sensation, looked towards his friend. He bore it with noble indifference, and she would have imagined that Bingley had received his sanction to be happy, had she not seen his eyes likewise turned towards Mr Darcy, with an expression of half-laughing alarm. He showed an admiration for Jane which persuaded Elizabeth that, if left wholly to himself, Jane's happiness and his own would be speedily secured. Mr Darcy was almost as far from her as the table could divide them. She hoped that the evening would afford some opportunity of bringing them together.

Later, she was pouring out the coffee and Jane was in charge of the tea, so when the gentlemen came in from the dining room to the drawing room there was no room near her. Darcy walked away. She followed him with her eyes, envied everyone to whom he spoke, and then was angry with herself for being so silly!

"A man who has once been refused! How could I be foolish enough to expect a renewal of his love?"

She was a little revived, however, by his bringing back his coffee cup himself; and she seized the opportunity of asking after his sister, but could think of nothing more to say. If he wanted to talk to her he might have better success. He stood by her, however, for some minutes, in silence, and at last walked way.

---

repaired: went
sanction: permission

"Well, girls," said Mrs Bennet as soon as the guests had left. "I think everything has passed off uncommonly well. And, my dear Jane, I never saw you look in greater beauty. Mrs Long said so too, for I asked her whether you did not. She said besides, 'Ah! Mrs Bennet, we shall have her at Netherfield at last.' "

A few days after their visit Mr Bingley called again, and alone. His friend had left that morning for London, but was to return in ten days' time. Mr Bingley was in remarkably good spirits. Mrs Bennet invited him to dine with them but he was engaged elsewhere. However, he consented to come on the next day, and came in such very good time that the ladies were none of them dressed. "My dear Jane, make haste and hurry down. Come, be quick, be quick," cried Mrs Bennet. But Jane would not be prevailed upon to go down without one of her sisters.

The same anxiety to get them by themselves was visible again in the evening. After tea, Mr Bennet retired to the library, and Mary went upstairs. Mrs Bennet started winking at Elizabeth and Catherine. Elizabeth would not observe her; and when at last Kitty did, she very innocently said, "What is the matter, mamma? What do you keep winking at me for? What am I to do?"

"Nothing, child, nothing. I did not wink at you." She then sat still five minutes longer; but, unable to waste such a precious occasion, she suddenly got up, and saying to Kitty, "Come here, my love, I want to speak to you," took her out of the room. Jane instantly gave a look at Elizabeth which showed her distress. As was expected, Mrs Bennet soon called Elizabeth. Though she was forced to go, Elizabeth made no attempt to reason with her mother, but remained quietly in the hall till she and Kitty were out of sight, then returned to the drawing room.

Mr Bennet and Mr Bingley spent the next morning together shooting. The latter was much more agreeable than his companion expected. There was nothing arrogant or foolish in Bingley's behaviour that could provoke his ridicule, or disgust him into silence so he was more communicative, and less eccentric than the other had ever seen him. Bingley of course returned with him to dinner. Elizabeth had a letter to write, and since the others were to sit down to cards, she went out of the room. But on returning to the room, she perceived her sister and Bingley standing together as if engaged in earnest conversation. The faces of both, as they hastily turned round and moved away from each other, would have told all. Bingley suddenly whispered a few words to her sister and ran out of the room.

Jane instantly embraced Elizabeth and acknowledged that she was the happiest creature in the world.

"It is too much!" she added, "by far too much. Oh! why is not everybody as happy."

Elizabeth's congratulations were given with a sincerity, a warmth, a delight, which words could but poorly express.

"I must go instantly to my mother," cried Jane. "I would not on any account trifle with her affectionate anxiety. He has gone to my father already." She then hastened away to her mother, who was sitting upstairs with Kitty. In a few minutes, Elizabeth was joined by Bingley, whose conference with her father had been short and to the purpose. Coming up to her, he claimed the good wishes and affection of a sister. Elizabeth honestly and heartily expressed her delight in the prospect of their relationship, and they shook hands with great cordiality.

It was an evening of no common delight to them all. Jane's happiness made her look prettier than ever. Kitty smiled and hoped her turn was coming soon. Mrs Bennet could not find words warm enough to satisfy her feelings; and when Mr Bennet joined them for supper, his voice and manner plainly showed how really happy he was. Not a word, however, passed

---

eccentric: peculiar, unusual

his lips about the subject till their visitors took his leave for the night. Then he turned to his daughter and said,

"Jane, I congratulate you. You will be a very happy woman."

Jane went to him instantly, kissed him, and thanked him for his goodness.

Bingley, from this time, was of course, a daily visitor at Longbourn. The situation in the Longbourn family could not be long a secret. Mrs Bennet whispered it to Mrs Philips, who did the same to all her neighbours in Meryton; and the Bennets were speedily pronounced to be the luckiest family in the world.

19

LADY CATHERINE'S VISIT

About a week later, as Bingley and the ladies of the family were sitting together in the dining room, they heard the sound of a carriage, and saw it driving up. Neither the carriage nor the livery of the servants was familiar to them; and so Bingley instantly persuaded Miss Bennet to walk with him into the shrubbery.

What was their astonishment when Lady Catherine de Bourgh entered the room, with an air more than usually ungracious, made no other reply to Elizabeth's greetings except by nodding, and sat down without saying a word.

After sitting for a moment, she said very stiffly, to Elizabeth, "That lady, I suppose, is your mother?"

Elizabeth replied that she was.

"You have a very small park here," said Lady Catherine, "and this must be a most inconvenient room for the evening in summer."

Mrs Bennet, all amazement, begged her ladyship to take some refreshment. But after a few ungracious remarks Lady Catherine rose and asked Elizabeth to take a walk with her in the copse by the lawn. Elizabeth obeyed. She was greatly

---

livery: special dress or uniform worn by servants in a well-to-do household, especially in the past

copse: a small area of trees, smaller than a wood

surprised, but determined to make no effort at conversation with a woman who was now more than usually insolent and disagreeable. As soon as they entered the copse, Lady Catherine began.

"You can be at no loss, Miss Bennet, to understand the reason of my journey here. Your own heart, your own conscience must tell you why I come."

Elizabeth looked at her in utter astonishment, and replied that she was not able to account for the honour of seeing Lady Catherine there.

"Miss Bennet," her ladyship continued in an angry tone. "A report of a most alarming nature reached me two days ago, that you would, in all likelihood, be soon united to my nephew, Mr Darcy. Though I *know* it must be a scandalous falsehood, I instantly resolved to make my feelings known to you."

"If you believe it impossible to be true," said Elizabeth, colouring with astonishment and disdain. "I wonder you took the trouble of coming so far. What could Your Ladyship propose by it?"

"At once to insist upon having such a report universally contradicted."

"Your coming to Longbourn, to see me and my family," said Elizabeth coolly, "will be rather a confirmation of it."

"This is not to be borne. Miss Bennet, I insist on being satisfied. Has my nephew made you an offer of marriage?"

"Your Ladyship has declared it to be impossible."

"It ought to be so; it must be so, while he retains the use of his reason. But *your* arts and allurements may have made him forget what he owes to himself and to all his family. You may have drawn him in."

"If I have, I shall be the last person to confess it."

---

disdain: scorn
allurements: attractions, charms

"Miss Bennet, I have not been accustomed to such language as this, I am almost the nearest relation he has in the world, and am entitled to know all his dearest concerns."

"But you are not entitled to know mine: nor will such behaviour as this ever induce me to be explicit."

"Let me be rightly understood. Mr Darcy is engaged to my *daughter*. Now, what have you to say?"

"Only this! that if he is so, you can have no reason to suppose he will make an offer to me."

Lady Catherine hesitated for a moment and then replied.

"The engagement between them is of a peculiar kind. From their infancy they have been intended for each other. It was the favourite wish of *his* mother, as well as of hers. Do you have no regard for the wishes of his friends?"

"But what is that to me? If there is no other objection to my marrying your nephew, I shall certainly not be kept from it, by knowing that his mother and aunt wished him to marry Miss de Bourgh. If I am Mr Darcy's choice, why may I not accept him?"

"Because honour, decorum, prudence, nay, interest, forbid it. You will be slighted and despised by everyone connected with him."

"These are heavy misfortunes," replied Elizabeth, "But the wife of Mr Darcy must have such sources of happiness attached to her situation, that she could have no cause to repine."

"My daughter and my nephew are formed for each other. They are descended, on the maternal side, from the same noble line; and on the fathers', from respectable and ancient families. What is to divide them? The upstart pretensions of a young woman without family, connections, or fortune? But it must

---

decorum: right and proper behaviour
repine: be discontented

not, shall not be! If you are sensible, you would not wish to quit the sphere in which you have been brought up."

"In marrying your nephew, I should not consider myself as quitting that sphere. He is a gentleman; I am a gentleman's daughter: so far we are equal."

"True, you *are* a gentleman's daughter. But who was your mother? Who are your uncles and aunts? Do not imagine me ignorant of their condition."

"Whatever my connections may be," said Elizabeth, "if your nephew does not object to them, they can be nothing to *you*."

"Tell me once for all, are you engaged to him?"

Though Elizabeth did not want to answer the question, she could not but say, after a moment's thought,

"I am not."

Lady Catherine seemed pleased.

"And you will promise me never to enter into such an engagement?"

"I will make no promise of the kind."

"Miss Bennet. I am shocked and astonished. I shall not go away till you have given me the assurance I require."

"And I certainly *never* shall give it. How far your nephew might approve of your interference in his affairs, I cannot tell; but you have certainly no right to concern yourself in mine—I must beg, therefore, to be questioned no further on the subject."

"Not so hasty, if you please. I know all about your younger sister's infamous elopement. Is *such* a girl to be my nephew's sister? Is her husband, who is the son of his late father's steward, to be his brother?"

"You can *now* have nothing further to say," Elizabeth resentfully answered. "You have insulted me by every possible method. I must beg to return to the house."

"Unfeeling, selfish girl! You are then resolved to have him?"

"I have said no such thing. I am only resolved to act in that manner, which will, in my own opinion, constitute my happiness, without reference to you or to any person so wholly unconnected with me."

"Very well. I shall now know how to act. But depend upon it, I will carry my point."

At the door of the carriage, turning hastily round, Lady Catherine added.

"I take no leave of you, Miss Bennet. I send no compliments to your mother. You deserve no such attention. I am seriously displeased."

Elizabeth made no answer but walked quietly into the house. Her mother impatiently met her at the door to ask why Lady Catherine did not come in.

"I suppose she had nothing particular to say to you, Lizzy?" she asked.

Elizabeth was forced into a little falsehood here; for to acknowledge the substance of their conversation was impossible.

20

Darcy and Elizabeth

Instead of receiving any letter of excuse from his friend, as Elizabeth half expected, Mr Bingley brought Mr Darcy with him to Longbourn before many days had passed. The gentlemen arrived early; and Bingley, who wanted to be alone with Jane, proposed their all walking out. Bingley and Jane lagged behind. Kitty presently stopped to call on Maria Lucas. When Elizabeth was alone with Mr Darcy, she resolved to thank him for his generous help with Lydia and said.

"Mr Darcy, I am a very selfish creature; and for the sake of giving relief to my own feelings, care not how much I may be wounding yours. I can no longer help thanking you for your infinite kindness to my poor sister."

"I am sorry, exceedingly sorry," replied Darcy, in a tone of surprise and emotion, "that you have been informed of what may, in a mistaken light, have given you uneasiness. I did not think Mrs Gardiner was so little to be trusted."

"You must not blame my aunt. Lydia's thoughtlessness first betrayed to me that you had been concerned in the matter. Let me thank you again and again, in the name of all my family, for that generous compassion which induced you to take so much trouble, and bear so much mortification, for the sake of discovering them."

"If you *will* thank me," he replied, "let it be for yourself alone. Your *family* owe me nothing. Much as I respect them, I believe I thought only of *you*."

Elizabeth was too much embarrassed to say a word. After a short pause her companion added: "You are too generous to trifle with me. If your feelings are still what they were last April, tell me so at once. *My* affections and wishes are unchanged; but one word from you will silence me on this subject for ever."

Elizabeth, feeling the awkwardness and anxiety of his situation, now forced herself to speak; and immediately, though not very fluently, gave him to understand that her sentiments had undergone so great a change, as to make her receive with gratitude and pleasure his present assurances. The happiness which this reply produced was such as he had probably never felt before; and he expressed himself on the occasion as sensibly and as warmly as a man violently in love can be supposed to do.

They walked on, without knowing in what direction. She learnt that they were indebted for their present good understanding to the efforts of his aunt, who *did* call on him in her return through London and inform him of their meeting. Unluckily for her ladyship, the effect of her words had been exactly the opposite.

"It taught me to hope," said he, "I knew enough of your disposition to be certain that, had you been absolutely decided against me, you would have said so to Lady Catherine frankly and openly."

Elizabeth coloured and laughed as she replied, "Yes, you know enough of my *frankness* to believe me capable of *that*."

"What did you say of me that I did not deserve? For though your accusations were ill-founded, my behaviour to you at the time merited the severest reproof. It was unpardonable. I shall never forget when you said 'had you behaved in a more gentleman-like manner'. Those were your words. You do not know how they have tortured me."

"Oh! do not repeat what I then said. I assure you that I have long been most heartily ashamed of it?"

Darcy mentioned his letter. "Did it," said he, "*soon* make you think better of me?"

She explained what its effect on her had been, and how, gradually, all her former prejudices had been removed. "Let us put aside all disagreeable recollections in our present happiness," Elizabeth said.

"Painful recollections will intrude, which ought not to be repelled. I have been a selfish being all my life. As a child, I was taught what was *right*, but I was not taught to correct my temper. I was given good principles, but left to follow them in pride and conceit. Unfortunately an only son, I was spoiled by my parents, who, though good themselves, allowed me to be selfish and overbearing, to care for none beyond my own family circle. Such I was and such I might still have been but for you, dearest, loveliest Elizabeth! You taught me a lesson, hard indeed at first, but most advantageous. You showed me how insufficient were all my pretensions to please a woman worthy of being pleased."

After walking several miles in a leisurely manner, and too busy to know anything about it, they found at last, on examining their watches, that it was time to be at home.

"What could have become of Mr Bingley and Jane!" was a wonder which introduced the discussion of *their* affairs. Darcy was delighted with their engagement of which his friend had informed him.

"I must ask whether you were surprised," said Elizabeth.

"Not at all, when I went away, I felt that it would soon happen. On the evening before my going to London," said he, "I made a confession to Bingley. I told him of all that had occurred to make my former interference in his affairs absurd

---

repelled: driven back
overbearing: wanting to force one's will on others
pretensions: claims to merit and importance

and impertinent. His surprise was great. I told him, moreover, that I believed myself mistaken in supposing, as I had done, that your sister was indifferent to him. I felt no doubt of their happiness together."

Elizabeth could not help smiling at his easy manner of directing his friend.

"Did you speak from your own observation," said she, "when you told him that my sister loved him, or merely from my information last spring?"

"I had narrowly observed her, during the two visits which I had lately made here, and I was convinced of her affection. I was obliged to confess to Bingley that your sister had been in town three months last winter, and that I had purposely kept it from him. He was angry, but he has heartily forgiven me now."

They continued the conversation till they reached the house. In the hall they parted.

---

impertinent: rude

21

A HAPPY ENDING

"Good gracious!" cried Mrs Bennet, as she stood at a window the next morning, "if that disagreeable Mr Darcy is not coming here again with our dear Bingley! Lizzy, you must walk out with him again, that he may not be in Bingley's way." Elizabeth could hardly help laughing at so convenient a proposal; yet was really vexed that her mother should be always calling him disagreeable.

As soon as they entered, Bingley looked at her so expressively, and shook hands with such warmth, as left no doubt of his knowledge of the situation.

"I advise Mr Darcy, and Lizzy, and Kitty," said Mrs Bennet, "to walk to Oakham Mount this morning. Mr Darcy has never seen the view."

"It may do well for the others," replied Mr Bingley, "but I am sure it will be too much for Kitty. Won't it, Kitty?"

Kitty owned that she had rather stay at home. Darcy professed a great curiosity to see the view from the Mount, and Elizabeth silently consented. During their walk, it was resolved that Mr Bennet's consent should be asked in the course of the evening. Elizabeth would ask her mother's.

In the evening, soon after Mr Bennet withdrew to the library, Elizabeth saw Darcy rise also and follow him, and her agitation was extreme. She did not fear her father's opposition, but he was going to be made unhappy. That *she*, his favourite child, should be distressing him by her choice, should be filling him with fear and regret in disposing of her, was a wretched reflection. She sat in misery until Mr Darcy appeared again and was relieved by his smile. When he whispered, "Go to your father," she was gone directly.

Her father was walking about the room, looking grave and anxious. "Lizzy," said he, "what are you doing? Are you out of your senses to be accepting this man? Have you not always hated him?"

How earnestly did she then wish that her former opinions had been more reasonable, her expressions more moderate! She assured him, with some confusion, of her attachment to Mr Darcy.

"We all know him to be a proud, unpleasant sort of man; but this would be nothing if you really liked him."

"I do, I do like him," she replied, with tears in her eyes. "I love him. Indeed he has no improper pride. He is perfectly amiable. You do not know what he really is; then pray do not pain me by speaking of him in such terms."

"Lizzy," said her father, "I have given him my consent. I now give it to *you*, if you are resolved on having him. But let me advise you to think better of it. I know your disposition, Lizzy. I know that you would not be happy, unless you truly esteemed your husband and looked up to him. My child, let me not have the grief of seeing you unable to respect your partner in life. You do not know what you are about."

Elizabeth was earnest and solemn in her reply. She told him of the gradual change in her feelings, how his affection was not the work of a day, but had stood the test of many months' suspense. She recounted all his good qualities and finally reconciled her father to the match.

"Well, my dear," said he, when she had stopped talking, "If this be the case he deserves you. I could not have parted with you, my Lizzy, to anyone less worthy."

To complete the favourable impression, she then told him what Mr Darcy had voluntarily done for Lydia. He heard her with astonishment.

"This is an evening of wonders, indeed! And so, Darcy did everything; made up the match, gave the money, paid the fellow's debts, and got him his commission! So much the better! Had it been your uncle, I must and *would* have paid him; but these violent young lovers carry everything their own way. I shall offer to pay him tomorrow. He will rant and storm about his love for you, and that will be the end of the matter!"

He allowed her at last to go, saying, as she left the room, "If any young men come for Mary or Kitty, send them in, for I am quite at leisure."

When her mother went up to her dressing room at night Elizabeth followed her, and made the important announcement. Its effect was most extraordinary. Mrs Bennet sat quite still, and unable to say anything. Nor was it for many, many minutes that she could comprehend what she heard. She began at length to recover.

"Good gracious! Lord bless me! only think! dear me! Mrs Darcy! Who would have thought it? Oh, my sweetest Lizzy! How rich and how great you will be! What jewels, what carriages you will have! Jane's is nothing to it, I am so pleased, so happy! Such a charming man: so handsome! So tall! Oh, my dear Lizzy! Pray apologise for my having disliked him so much before. Dear, dear Lizzy! A house in town! Everything that is charming! Three daughters married! Ten thousand a year! Oh, Lord! What will become of me? I shall go distracted."

Elizabeth was afraid of what her mother's behaviour to the gentleman himself might be. But the next day passed off much better than she expected; for Mrs Bennet luckily stood in such awe of her intended son-in-law that she did not venture to speak to him, unless it was in her power to offer him any attention.

Happy for Mrs Bennet was the day on which she parted from her two most deserving daughters. It may be guessed with what delighted pride she afterwards visited Mrs Bingley, and talked of Mrs Darcy. Mr Bennet missed his second daughter exceedingly; his affection for her drew him oftener from home than anything else could do. He delighted in going to Pemberley, especially when he was least expected.

Mr Bingley and Jane remained at Netherfield only a year. So near a vicinity to her mother and Meryton relations was not desirable even to *his* easy temper, or *her* affectionate heart. The darling wish of the sisters was then gratified; Bingley bought an estate in the neighbouring county to Derbyshire; and Jane and Elizabeth, in addition to every other source of happiness, were within thirty miles of each other.

Kitty spent most of her time with her two elder sisters. In society so superior to what she had so generally known, her improvement was great. Removed from the influence of Lydia's example, she became, by proper attention and management, less irritable, less ignorant and less stupid. Though Mrs Wickham frequently invited her to come and stay with her, with the promise of balls and young men, her father would never consent to her going.

Mary was the only daughter who remained at home. As Mrs Bennet was always quite unable to sit alone, Mary had to give up her reading and keep her company. She was no longer humiliated by comparisons between her sisters' beauty and her own, and she began to enjoy her outings.

As for Wickham and Lydia, their characters suffered no revolution from the marriage of her sisters. He bore with composure the knowledge that Elizabeth must now become acquainted with whatever of his ingratitude and falsehood had before been unknown to her. He was not without hope that Darcy might yet be prevailed upon to make his fortune. But Lydia's requests were firmly rejected by Elizabeth. Such relief, however, as was possible by practising economy in her own private expenses, she always sent them; for Jane or she was always being asked for assistance in paying their bills.

Miss Bingley was deeply mortified by Darcy's marriage; but as she thought it advisable to retain the right to visit Pemberley, she dropped all her resentment, was fonder than ever of Georgiana, almost as attentive to Darcy as before and paid off every arrear of civility to Elizabeth. Pemberley was now Georgiana's home; and the attachment of the sisters was exactly what Darcy had hoped to see. Georgiana had the highest opinion in the world of Elizabeth. At first she often listened with an astonishment bordering on alarm at Elizabeth's lively, sportive manner of talking to her brother, since her own respect for him almost overcame her affection.

Lady Catherine was extremely indignant about the marriage of her nephew. The language of her letter was so very abusive, especially of Elizabeth, that for some time all communications were at an end. But at length Elizabeth persuaded Darcy to overlook the offence and seek a reconciliation, and after a little further resistance on the part of the aunt, she condescended to visit them at Pemberely.

With the Gardiners they were always on the most intimate terms. Darcy, as well as Elizabeth, really loved them; and both always felt the warmest gratitude towards the persons who, by bringing her into Derbyshire, had been the means of uniting them.

---

arrear of civility: what was owing in politeness

Exercises

Chapters 1–3

As you read

1. What news did Mrs Bennet give Mr Bennet?
2. Why was Mrs Bennet interested in their new neighbour at Netherfield Park?
3. Why did Mr Bennet have a soft corner for Elizabeth? What did he feel about the other daughters?
4. Who was Darcy? Why was Elizabeth annoyed with him?
5. How did Jane feel about Bingley?

Looking at language

You can make uncountable nouns singular by using certain phrases such as those given in the box. Now fill in the blanks with appropriate phrases and complete the sentences.

spell of, piece of, bit of, flash of, breath of, fit of, clap of, shower of

1. We had a good .... summer last year.
2. John was frightened on hearing a .... thunder.
3. There was a .... lightning in the sky.
4. The sudden .... rain spoilt the outing.
5. We wanted a .... fresh air so we opened the windows.
6. My father was in a .... anger when he saw me returning home late.
7. I heard an interesting .... news from my friend.
8. He revealed a really useful .... information yesterday.

Developing your reading

Elizabeth took an intense dislike for Darcy at their very first meeting. Do you think she was justified in doing so? Discuss this with your friends and teacher in class.

Chapters 4&5

As you read

1. How did Miss Bingley and Mrs Hurst regard Jane and Mrs Bennet?
2. Do you think Darcy found Elizabeth attractive? How do you know?
3. Why did Mrs Bennet send Jane to Netherfield on horseback?
4. How did Elizabeth feel when she heard Jane was ill? What did she do?
5. Who was Mr Collins? Why did he want to marry one of the Bennet daughters?
6. Who was Wickham? What did he tell Elizabeth about Darcy?

Looking at language

A. Match the words with the correct phrases.

	A	*B*
1.	a blade of	grain
2.	a handful of	toothpaste
3.	a tube of	soap
4.	a bar of	coal
5.	a lump of	grass

B. "His guilt and descent appear by your account to be the same," said Elizabeth angrily.

Another way to show the manner of speaking is to use a verb that indicates the person's mood or the expression on his face.

"Excuse the interference," she sneered, "it was kindly meant."

Match the utterances on the left to their suitable reporting verbs on the right.

1. "She is not beautiful enough to tempt me,"	she frowned.
2. "You will have a charming mother-in-law,"	grinned Mr Bennet.
3. "I hope Mr Bingley will like it, Lizzy,"	she laughed.
4. "I think him very disagreeable,"	he scoffed.
5. "And is this all? I had expected at least that the pigs had got into the garden,"	she sneered.

CHAPTERS 6&7

As you read

1. To whom did Mr Collins propose at first? Why?
2. Describe Mr and Mr Bennet's reactions to Mr Collins's proposal.
3. How did Mr Collins behave when Elizabeth turned down his offer?
4. Why was Jane upset when she received a letter from Miss Bingley?
5. How did Charlotte attract Mr Collins? What were her reasons for marrying him?

Looking at language

A. Write the opposites of the words given below using negative prefixes.

Example: decent – indecent

1. sensitive ....
2. responsible ....
3. honest ....
4. obedient ....
5. tolerant ....

6. literate ....
7. fair ....
8. tidy ....
9. grateful ....
10. efficient ....

B. Use any five words with their negative prefixes in sentences of your own.

Chapters 8&9

As you read

1. Who were Mr and Mrs Gardiner?
2. Why did Elizabeth go to London?
3. Who was Lady Catherine? What did Elizabeth think of Lady Catherine and her daughter? Why?
4. How did Lady Catherine behave at Rosings? Why was Elizabeth annoyed with her?

Looking at language

A. There are some words which only occur in the plural, *Example:* scissors, pliers, jeans, pyjamas, shorts, trousers etc.

Now fill in the blanks with such words given in the box.

lodgings, goods, authorities, headquarters, acoustics, contents, outskirts, stairs, proceeds, whereabouts.

1. When one gets transferred to a new town it is difficult to find ....
2. The.............of the concert were given to the relief fund.
3. I somehow managed to get accommodation on the .... of the city.
4. The military............. were greatly puzzled at the cause of the crash.
5. The.............of the ministry were shifted due to security reasons.

6. The.............in the auditorium were remarkable.
7. The.............were steep and difficult to climb.
8. The ....of the official were not known.
9. The.............were delivered on time
10. The............. of the house were auctioned.

Developing your reading

Why do you think Lady Catherine asked Elizabeth all these questions? Was she just curious or did she want to find out something?

CHAPTERS 10&11

As you read

1. Who was Colonel Fitzwilliam?
2. What did he reveal about Darcy's opinion of Jane? How did Elizabeth feel about it?
3. How did Mr Darcy propose to Elizabeth?
4. Why did Elizabeth turn down the proposal?

Looking at language

A. Look at these phrases. Match the phrases with the words to form similes.

Example: as heavy as lead.

	A	*B*
1.	as hard as	an arrow
2.	as deaf as	a beetroot
3.	as quick as	snow
4.	as red as	a cucumber
5.	as white as	iron
6.	as cool as	a post
7.	as brown as	a feather
8.	as mad as	brass
9.	as bold as	a berry
10.	as light as	a hatter

B. Fill in the blanks with appropriate similes.
   1. Anamika is crazy. She is as mad as.............
   2. The old man's hair was as white..............
   3. You will have to speak louder. She is as deaf as..........
   4. He ran very fast. He was as quick as..............
   5. The student was very daring. He was as bold as..........

Chapters 12&13

As you read

1. How did Mr Darcy justify his behaviour towards Jane and Mr Wickham?
2. What did Elizabeth conclude after reading Darcy's letter? Did she agree with him?
3. Do you think Elizabeth's feelings towards Darcy underwent a change? How do you know? Whom did she blame for Jane's humiliation?
4. When did Elizabeth break the news about Wickham to Jane? What did she reveal to Jane?
5. Why was Wickham alarmed?

Looking at language

A. Look at these idioms and their meanings given below. Match those in *A* to their correct meanings in *B*. Then use them in sentences of your own.

A	*B*
1. down in the dumps	stay calm
2. like a bear with a sore head	be fooled
3. be in high spirits	not feeling very well
4. be on cloud nine	depressed or sad
5. as fit as a fiddle	feeling irritable
6. a bit under the weather	enjoying things
7. get carried away	extremely thrilled
8. keep a cool head	in very good health

B. Read the first paragraph of Darcy's letter to Elizabeth on page 65. The style of writing is old fashioned.

Rewrite the paragraph in the way it would be written today. You could begin by using any of the options below or any other way you like.

Dear Ms Bennet,
Please don't be surprised by my letter...
or
Dear Ms Bennet,
I hope this letter will not come as a surprise to you...

Developing your reading

"And how much I have to conceal," thought Elizabeth. What were the things that Elizabeth had to conceal? How much did she conceal?

Chapters 14&16

As you read

1. What reasons did Mr Bennet have for marrying Mrs Bennet? What was the result?
2. What was Elizabeth's impression of Mr Darcy when she visited Pemberley?
3. Write in a sentence or two Elizabeth's opinion of Miss Darcy.
4. When Elizabeth visited Mr Darcy's house how did Miss Bingley behave?
5. What had Lydia done to make Elizabeth so anxious? Describe Elizabeth's reaction on reading Jane's letter.
6. Describe Mrs Bennet's feelings about Lydia's elopement.

Looking at language

A. Look at these idioms. Work out the meanings and write them out. Use a dictionary if necessary.
   1. to take a back seat

2. to take the bull by the horns
3. to lay one's cards on the table
4. the tide has turned
5. to bury the hatchet
6. to go a long way
7. to go back to square one
8. to be on tenterhooks
9. to toe the line
10. to go hand in hand

B. Pick out five adjectives from the chapter that describe Pemberley House and the woods.

Chapters 17–21

As you read

1. How did Lydia behave on her arrival home after her marriage?
2. How did Mrs Gardiner's letter raise Elizabeth's respect for Darcy?
3. What light does the conversation between Elizabeth and Lady Catherine throw on their respective characters?
4. Briefly describe how Darcy proposed to Elizabeth at Longbourn?
5. Where did Jane and Elizabeth settle down after marriage? Who visited them often?

Looking at language

A. Look at these notices. Expand them into sentences using simple, everyday English.

Example: Do not alight from the bus while it is in motion.

Don't get off the bus while it is moving.
Feeding animals strictly prohibited.
Trespassers will be prosecuted.
You ....

People ....
Smoking prohibited
No vacancies here
No admission to unaccompanied minors
You ....
There ....
Young ....

B. Match the meanings on the left with those on the right.

A	*B*
1. prosecute	not to do something
2. a penalty	someone who enters a place without permission
3. a trespassers	forbid something
4. prohibit	a punishment
5. a minor	bring a legal case against someone
6. refrain	a young person under the age of eighteen

Developing your reading

After her marriage to Darcy, Elizabeth writes to her friend Charlotte about her courtship and eventual marriage to him. Imagine you are Elizabeth and complete this letter to Charlotte.

Pemberley,
10th August

My Dear Charlotte,

You probably are surprised that I am married to the man whom I so intensely disliked. I thought I should tell you how it all happened . . .

Your affectionate friend,

Lizzy.